Journey to a Cure

Journey to a Cure

When traditional medical methods failed, a mother helped her son defeat several mental disorders using alternative treatments

Emily L. Dillon

Createspace Independent Publishing Platform
North Charleston, SC

THE INFORMATION AND ADVICE PRESENTED IN THIS BOOK ARE NOT MEANT TO SUBSTITUTE FOR THE ADVICE OF YOUR PHYSICIAN OR OTHER TRAINED HEALTHCARE PROFESSIONAL. YOU ARE ADVISED TO CONSULT WITH HEALTHCARE PROFESSIONALS WITH REGARD TO ALL MATTERS THAT MAY REQUIRE MEDICAL ATTENTION OR DIAGNOSIS AND TO CHECK WITH A PHYSICIAN BEFORE ADMINISTERING OR UNDERTAKING ANY COURSE OF TREATMENT OR DIET.

TO PROTECT THE PRIVACY OF THE PEOPLE WHOSE STORIES ARE SHARED IN THIS BOOK, MANY NAMES AND SOME IDENTIFYING INFORMATION HAVE BEEN CHANGED.

COPYRIGHT © 2017 BY EMILY L. DILLON

ALL RIGHTS RESERVED. THIS BOOK OR ANY PORTION THEREOF MAY NOT BE REPRODUCED OR USED IN ANY MANNER WHATSOEVER WITHOUT THE EXPRESS WRITTEN PERMISSION OF THE PUBLISHER EXCEPT FOR THE USE OF BRIEF QUOTATIONS IN A BOOK REVIEW.

PRINTED IN THE UNITED STATES OF AMERICA

FIRST PRINTING, 2017

ISBN-13: 978-1979367714

ISBN-10: 197936771X

LIBRARY OF CONGRESS CONTROL NUMBER: 2017917222

CREATESPACE INDEPENDENT PUBLISHING PLATFORM, NORTH CHARLESTON, SC

FIRST EDITION

This book is dedicated to my husband Steve who is an amazing husband and father. I could not have done what I did without his support.

And to

My best friend Jenn who cried with me, celebrated victories and knew when what I really needed was a glass of wine or two!

And to

My Dad who had the ultimate faith in me, encouraged me to never give up and listened to me talk about what I had discovered for countless hours.

And to

My son Matthew, who brought fun and silliness into our house and never gave up on his brother.

And to

Jesus Christ, who gave me strength, courage and wisdom.

And to

To my son David, who did everything I asked no matter how hard it was on him and never lost faith that God would see him through.

Contents

	A Note About the Author	1
1	The Early Years – Birth to Age 6	2
2	First Through Third Grade	12
3	Fourth Through Fifth Grade	23
4	Sixth Grade	43
5	First Half of Seventh Grade	61
6	Second Half of Seventh Grade	91
7	Eighth Grade	105
8	First Half of Ninth Grade	116
9	Second Half of Ninth Grade	128
10	Tenth and Eleventh Grade	147
11	Today	154

A NOTE ABOUT THE AUTHOR

Emily L. Dillon never expected to write a book, but her struggle to help her oldest son overcome severe mental and behavioral disorders inspired her to do so. She hopes her experiences researching a natural cure for her son's mental health and behavior problems will help other families receive the assistance they need without enduring her difficult journey.

She and her husband, Steve, have two sons, David and Matthew. She holds a college degree and loves cooking, reading, gardening, and savoring a glass of wine. She volunteers as a mentor for a children's charity.

Chapter 1

*The Early Years -
Birth Through Age 6*

Steve and I were both 30 when we met. It was a blind date for us, but pretty much love at first sight. We had so much in common and on our first date we even discussed both wanting three children. We were engaged in a little over a year and married two years from the day we met. We bought our first house a few months later and when we showed our friends, everyone thought it was weird because it was too big for just the two of us. However, we were planning for our future family and hoped to never move. We wanted to stay in the same home where we would make all our family memories. We decided on our two year anniversary that it was time to start a family and I got pregnant that month. We couldn't have been more excited! There was nothing out of the ordinary during my pregnancy and we chose not to find out the sex of the baby as we wanted to be surprised.

David came into this world in a fast and furious manner; little did we know that is how our lives would be for many years to come. He was one week late, but from the moment my water broke and contractions started he was born six hours later. It would have been a little sooner, but the cord was wrapped around his neck twice, so they had to stop contractions and deliver him by emergency C-section. His Apgar scores were low at birth, but normalized within a couple minutes. He was 7.5 pounds, 22 inches long and had a head of beautiful brown hair. We came home the next day.

Even though he was our first, it all seemed a little too easy in the beginning. He was happy most of the time and at six weeks was sleeping through the night. Sure, he cried when he was hungry, wet or cold like most babies, but he was easily consolable. He loved everyone and overall had a very easy disposition.

He met all of his benchmarks early, so there were no early signs of what was to come. He said his first word, "mama" on his nine-month anniversary and was walking two weeks later.

Being well aware of the controversial aspects of vaccines relative to neurological disorders among children, we chose to have David vaccinated, but did split them up so he didn't get quite as many at one time as was recommended. While some people blame vaccinations for their children's disorders, we do not feel they contributed to the problems we would later see in David.

As for diet, David was breastfed exclusively for six months and completely weaned by 14 months. He started on rice cereal at six months and moved onto baby food shortly after that. He was always a good eater and not picky at all.

By age one, David was running around the house and trying to get into everything. I didn't know it yet, but early signs of problems were starting to emerge. When he would get into something or do something I didn't want him to do I would tell him "no" and try to redirect him. His reaction was as if I had said and done nothing, like I didn't even exist. If I spoke to him, he completely ignored me and if I redirected him, he would go right back to what he was doing previously.

I started to think I must be doing something wrong, that somehow it was my parenting that was the problem. I talked to my parents and friends and got advice, but no matter what I did nothing changed. I just assumed we must be experiencing "the terrible twos" a little early. He still seemed really happy, he just didn't listen to any directions his Dad or I gave him.

By age two, we actually had David's hearing tested. In our opinion this just had to be why he didn't listen to us at all. The tests showed his hearing was absolutely normal. Our pediatrician said he was probably just strong willed.

I gave birth to our second son, Matthew, just after David's second birthday. He was the exact opposite of David, he was never happy, hardly ever slept, cried all the time and hated everyone but me. Dealing with a fussy baby and an obstinate two-year old that did what he wanted when he wanted no matter what anyone said or did was the beginning of the difficult years that lay ahead of us.

One year later, our fussy Matthew had transformed into an easy child, but David had gotten worse. By age three, we had started play dates and a few hours of preschool (I really needed a break a few hours per week,) but there were always conflicts. David didn't share well, he didn't want to play by the rules, and he didn't do what the teacher or other parents told him. He also was extremely competitive and was intensely upset if he didn't win. We tried talking to him, bribing him, spankings, time-outs, and nothing made any difference at all. Our pediatrician said it was just his age and he would probably grow out of it.

David did not play nice with his little brother. Matthew idolized him, but the only thing David seemed to want to do was make Matthew cry. He took his toys and ran away, he knocked over blocks that had been stacked up and by the age of four he began viciously hitting Matthew. I couldn't leave them alone more than six feet away from where I was standing. However, there were those infrequent moments where I would see a tender and kind heart in David. He would sometimes get his favorite book and he would have Matthew climb up onto his tiny lap and read to him. He also often would kiss him on the head and say "I love you" at bedtime. It was like I had a wonderful kid that was trapped behind something terrible and frightening.

Over the next two years, I noticed that Matthew had not been difficult at one, two or three years old. He listened to what we said, understood the word "no" and got along with other kids. After Matthew had been in preschool just a couple months his teacher commented on what a delight he was. I can't remember her exact words, but I was able to read between the lines and get the message that he was so different and so much easier than David had been. I started to fear that David's behavioral problems were more than just his age and a strong will.

David had started sucking his thumb as a tiny baby and at the time we thought it was so cute. He was able to soothe himself without having to find a pacifier, so it seemed like a good idea to let him do it. By the age of three he was sucking it excessively, so we started trying to discourage it, but he was determined to keep doing it. Over the next couple years we tried applying an anti-thumb sucking solution that tasted bad and tying a glove on his hand, but neither worked. We eventually forced him to stop by putting multiple Band-Aids around his thumbs and punished him if he tried to remove them. He immediately started licking his hands and then rubbing them on his face until it was chapped and raw.

By the age of four, he was having vivid nightmares about monsters a couple times a week. He would be terrified and generally unable to go back to sleep by himself. My husband and I took turns staying in his room, so he would go back to sleep, but if we even so much as moved an inch he would wake up again. His Dad made up the "monster dance" and did it in his room every night before bedtime to scare the monsters away. David would often want him to do it a dozen times.

By the age of six, living with David was exhausting. It would take us two hours to do homework that should have taken 10 – 15 minutes. He would roll around on the floor, put his head on the desk, or draw pictures on the homework page, anything, but the actual homework! He wasn't stupid, we knew he knew how to do it, he just didn't want to.

We couldn't get him to do anything without helping him. If we asked him to put a toy away he simply wouldn't do it. If we asked him to brush his teeth, he would play in the water or never even make to the bathroom. If we asked him to get his pajamas on, we would find him in his room playing. Every single task required us doing it with or for him.

Socially, our life was difficult. Most of our friends also had children of similar ages and every time we would get together with anyone there would always be a problem with David at the center of it. He had trouble sharing, he had specific demands (such as needing to go first, needing to have a certain color game piece, had to be in a certain position, etc.), he wanted to change the rules to benefit him and he absolutely had to win or he would throw a fit. When he didn't get his way he would often push or hit the other children. Even though he would be punished on the spot, nothing changed. We lost friends and in some cases were invited over less often. It was frustrating and heartbreaking at the same time.

Six was the age of the birthday parties, and most kids in a class invited everyone to their party. However, most of the time David would not be invited and he would be so hurt. We would try to explain to him that his behavior was to blame and he would cry and say "Mommy, I don't want to be bad." His sincerity in this statement would break my heart.

I felt like the only two emotions I had were anger and sadness. I was angry that our life was so difficult when it should have been so easy. I had an amazing husband with a good job, a nice house in a wonderful community, great friends and family and we all had abundant health, or so I thought. I should have been living the perfect life, but because David could not seem to control himself, everything was difficult. However, in addition to the anger, I felt a deep sadness because I knew David couldn't possibly be that happy always being in trouble, always being talked to, always being yelled at, and knowing his parents were seemingly never happy with him. I often cried myself to sleep.

Chapter 2
First Through Third Grade

David was already six by the beginning of first grade and he had team teachers. One taught two days and the other taught three days per week. David loved one and hated the other; he said she was mean. On "the mean teacher's" days, David did not want to go school. Within a couple weeks, I was getting emails that David was having trouble staying on task, was fidgety and couldn't stay in his seat. Homework remained a nightmare and I remember thinking that I would rather have a root canal then have to face another afternoon of it!

    The first week of January after the Christmas break, his teachers asked me to come in for a private meeting. They said David couldn't concentrate, didn't follow directions and even though there were no serious problems, he struggled to get along with other kids and often played alone at recess. One of the teachers said she kept a pocket of tootsie rolls to bribe him throughout the day. The other teacher punished him for not doing what he was supposed to, but either way nothing seemed to work. I told them about the problems we were having at home and they asked if we had spoken to our pediatrician. I said I had mentioned a few things over the years and he had said it was his age and strong will. I remember thinking "Why would I talk to my doctor about my child's bad behavior, it's not like it's a medical problem." They suggested I have David tested. My response was "tested for what?" They said they couldn't really say, but in their opinion he should "be tested." I pushed them and they indicated that he fit the profile of a child with ADHD (Attention Deficit Hyperactivity Disorder.)

> *Attention-deficit/hyperactivity disorder (ADHD) is a chronic condition that affects millions of children and often continues into adulthood. ADHD includes a combination of persistent problems, such as difficulty sustaining attention, hyperactivity and impulsive behavior.*

My first thought was "No way did my kid have that!! Other people's kids had those problems, but no way did mine!" After all, his Dad and I were both college graduates and no one in our families had ever had academic problems. However, as the next few days wore on, the thought that maybe this is why David was so uncontrollable started to cross my mind. Maybe there was a "cause," and if there was a "cause" maybe there was a "solution."

We saw our pediatrician about a week later and told him about our school meeting and what we were experiencing at home. He said it so calmly, like it was no big deal "sounds like ADHD." He handed me some papers and told me to go home and fill them out with my husband and then come back in a week or two.

The paperwork consisted of the *Conner's Parent Rating Scale (which* asks about the child's symptoms) and the Conner's *Teacher Rating Scale* (which is used to evaluate the child's symptoms in the classroom). On a scale from 0-3, (0-not at all, 1-just a little, 2-pretty much and 3-very much) we had to rate David on numerous categories such as:

- Excitable/impulsive
- Appears to lack leadership
- Restless in the squirmy sense
- Daydreams
- No sense of fair play

We struggled with the questionnaire. There were no descriptions of what normal was supposed to be, so we weren't sure if his daydreaming, for example, was just a little or very much compared to normal. There were no descriptions of what very much or very little meant in any category. Were we supposed to compare his behaviors to Matthew, to children who seemed very well behaved or to other children who did not seem well behaved? We did the best we could, but did not feel confident that our answers were accurate. They seemed subjective and more like opinions that could vary by one's current state of mind.

We turned in our parent rating questionnaire, along with the teachers rating into our pediatrician. He read over the answers for literally less than two minutes and said, "Looks like he has ADHD," and then started talking about prescription medications that could help. I felt like my head was spinning. I said, "Whoa, without examining my son and just going off of our and his teachers opinions about his behavior, you are diagnosing him with a neurological disorder?" He said that is how the diagnosis is done.

I went home feeling panicked and started researching some of the prescription medications he had mentioned. Most of them were classified as Schedule II substances and the possible side effects were serious and scary:

- sleep problems

- anxiety

- weight loss

- irritability

- increased violence

- painful erections that could last hours

- long term use could lead to dependency

My husband and I couldn't help but think that the side effects sounded worse than the behavioral symptoms. We also felt very uncomfortable that how we answered the questions on the Conner's Parent Rating scale was solely responsible for the diagnosis. We did, and still do like and respect our pediatrician, but the diagnosis process seemed like such a giant grey area to us. We requested, and received a referral to a pediatric psychiatrist (Dr. Franklin). We talked to Dr. Franklin about not wanting to have his diagnosis based on our opinions without knowing what normal really looked like. He agreed to meet with David and ask us questions that were specific and not so general. After three appointments, he said there were certainly signs of ADHD, but not enough in his opinion to start prescription medications. He said we should wait and see what happened over the next year or two. I immediately felt relief, I thought "David might not have a neurological problem and we might not have to face those scary medications!" However, by the time we got home, I couldn't help, but wonder if we were responsible for a diagnosis that seemed less scary to us. We had chosen our answers very carefully, never lied of course, but looking back now I feel we possibly down played some behaviors and made them seem less serious.

Over the next two years, I read several parenting books and we tried many different approaches to get David to listen and behave more appropriately. We also gave him Omega 3 + DHA supplements in the form of gummy bears which is supposed to support healthy brain development. We had small victories along the way, but for the most part, David continued to get worse.

Our school only gave "pass" or "no pass" grades through 3rd grade and David always passed. It seemed to us that he was fairly bright, but overall had no interest in school. Homework continued to be very challenging and teachers were continually telling us about his inability to follow directions, stay on task, etc.

By the end of third grade, David had a lot of trouble going to sleep. He could be absolutely exhausted and yet lay in bed for hours without being able to fall asleep. We increased the amount of time we read to him before bedtime, lowered the lights in the house, sang to him, but nothing seemed to help. His nightmares also continued, but changed from monsters to our pet cats being injured or his Dad and I disappearing. He often would yell downstairs a dozen times a night "Mommy, are you and Daddy still there?" We never ever left our kids at home alone, so we were always confused about why this scared him so much.

During this time, David started pulling his hair out until he was mostly bald. He had golf ball sized patches of hair missing all over his head. We asked him why he did it and he said he didn't know. We did everything seemingly possible to get him to stop, but nothing worked until we started keeping his hair super short, so he couldn't get ahold of it enough to yank it out. We later learned this is an anxiety based disorder called trichotillomania.

Trichotillomania - a compulsive desire to pull out one's hair.

David also started making faces such as a grimace for no apparent reason. It was as if he didn't even know he was doing it. He also licked his lips and the area around them so much that they were constantly chapped and raw.

Socially, David only had one friend, a neighbor boy named Timmy. Timmy was a really nice kid who seemed to be ok with letting David have his way most of the time. When he really didn't like something he would just leave, but he would be back the next day as if nothing had happened. He was a Godsend for David!

David hated his brother Matthew and never let us or him forget it. He always thought we loved Matthew more which is why I think he hated him so much. We did and said everything we could think of to change his mind, but nothing did the trick. Whether it was Christmas gifts or spending time with the boys, we always made sure things were equal between them. He said we were never fair when it came to disputes between them, so he started taking matters into his own hands and hitting Matthew as punishment for whatever he deemed unfair. He was extremely bossy and never took responsibility for his actions.

David started fights with Matthew multiple times in a day. He teased him, turned the TV off, flicked him in the back of the head, stole his stuff, etc. He did whatever he could to start a problem, so as soon as Matthew would react, he could retaliate. His fighting was way more aggressive and clearly aimed at hurting Matthew. We would always try to intervene, but often couldn't get there fast enough to stop the fight before it began.

Our house was not peaceful and it seemed like I was yelling all the time! Yelling was something I always hated and swore I wouldn't do and yet here I was behaving in a way I didn't like. Yelling didn't work any better than talking, yet somehow it seemed appropriate at the time. Everything I needed David to do (finish his homework, brush his teeth, change his clothes, leave his brother alone) required multiple requests usually ending with me doing it for him. My husband and I both felt frustrated, exhausted and hopeless.

Chapter 3
Fourth through Fifth Grade

David was 9 ½ when he started 4th grade and had moved up to middle school. The school was really cranking up the pace of learning compared to the past couple of years and David started struggling almost right away. In November, his teacher requested a conference. She said she had read his records from his prior teachers and that along with what she was seeing in her classroom made her certain David suffered from ADHD. She said she had taught many kids over the years with it and in her opinion he fit the profile exactly. She also said she thought he had it pretty bad. She thought David was pretty bright which is why he was able to pass from grade to grade in the past, but she didn't think his "brightness" was able to compensate for the ADHD anymore. She indicated her belief that from 4th grade on through future grades he would fall farther behind academically each year without medical intervention.

Since we were under new medical insurance, we had to make an appointment with a new Pediatrician (Dr. Hutchinson). We weren't able to be seen until January. David was initially diagnosed with an "adjustment disorder with mixed disturbance of emotions and conflict" and a secondary diagnosis of learning difficulties. We were referred to a clinical psychologist (Dr. Manchester) who after interviewing myself, my husband and David separately for an hour each, diagnosed David with ADHD, anxiety and a possible tic disorder.

ADHD (Attention Deficit Hyperactivity Disorder) – A brain disorder marked by an ongoing pattern in inattention and/or hyperactivity/impulsivity that interferes with functioning and development

Anxiety – A nervous disorder characterized by a state of excessive uneasiness and apprehension, typically with compulsive behavior or panic attack

Tics – Short lasting sudden movements (motor tics) or uttered sounds (vocal tics) that occur suddenly during normal activity. They are repetitive with numerous successive occurrences of the same action.

He recommended we start with a small dose of Ritalin and see how it goes. He said it was the entry level as far as stimulant based drugs go. He wanted us to give David one at breakfast to help in school and one when he got home from school to help with homework and behavior. We decided we wouldn't use them on weekends, school breaks or holidays to minimize his exposure to the drugs and hopefully lower his odds of getting one of the possible side effects.

Within three weeks of being on the Ritalin, David was worse. His attitude was 100% negative and he was completely filled with anger and frustration. He spent most of his energy trying to provoke his brother into lashing out, so we would be forced to punish Matthew. He constantly told his Dad and I how mean we were and that he knew we hated him. He also told us often how he wished he were dead. His teacher said that he had become more oppositional and could not get along with anyone. Our house felt more like a war zone than a home. My instincts were telling me that David's problems were far worse than ADHD and a little anxiety.

I shared my fears with Dr. Manchester and he said I needed to give it more time. He also wanted me to read a book about using a specific reward system to encourage desired behaviors and to attend ADHD classes. I read the book and my husband and I attended the classes and we tried to implement the things we learned, but it seemed to make little to no difference.

Two months later we were referred to a different clinical psychologist (Dr. Paul) who specialized in ADHD. He said he didn't think the small doses of Ritalin which generally only last two to three hours were enough. He recommended we move to Concerta which is a time released stimulant drug, lasting eight to twelve hours. We started with 18mg and that combined with the things we had learned from the book and the ADHD classes seemed to help some. David was less argumentative, bothered his brother fewer times per day and his teacher reported an improvement in school. He also stopped licking his hands and rubbing them on his face and we were able to let his hair grow out some as he didn't pull it out anymore. However, we noticed that he started touching his ear every time he asked us a question and he was having more trouble falling asleep.

By the beginning of 5th grade, the small improvements we seemed to have in 4th grade had just slipped away. David was obsessed with the thought that we didn't love him and that nothing in our house was fair. He hated Matthew with a passion and instigated fights and disagreements constantly. He was struggling in school both academically and socially. He was exhausted all the time because he had so much trouble falling asleep; the doctors said it was most likely a side effect of the Concerta. Additionally, his facial grimacing was getting worse.

Dr. Paul increased his Concerta dose to 27mgs and added on Ritalin for times when we thought he needed extra help with concentration or impulse control. He recommended a lava lamp and children's sleep CD to help with the sleep problems and wanted us to start family counselling.

In my heart, I knew lava lamps, sleep CDs and family counselling was not the answer, but I felt like I had to try everything. The counselor's focus was on changing our parenting style to make everything wonderful and rosy. He said that if we gave David an immediate time out every time he started to argue, he wouldn't argue anymore, that it would become a learned behavior. He had me read another book on how to parent a child with ADHD. He had us implement a ticket system where every time David had good behavior he would get a ticket and tickets could be redeemed for a treat. Good behavior was as basic as walking into a room with Matthew and not picking a fight with him immediately. He said this system of rewarding good behavior would reduce bad behavior. We also were instructed to do whatever David wanted for 20 minutes per day regardless of his behavior.

In spite of our lack of confidence that any of this would work, we gave it the old college try! My husband and I both sincerely did what was recommended to us for months, but nothing really changed. By November, David was pulling his hair out again and had to wear a baseball cap to school. He had started to blink a lot and stretch his mouth (tics). The blinks were like if someone told you to close your eyes as tight as you could, so tight your cheeks rise up under your eyes. The mouth stretches were like the biggest yawn you could do. He also started twisting his ear until it was cherry red.

I kept complaining that the treatments were not working and David was not getting better. We were then referred to a Pediatric

Psychiatrist (Dr. Dorrington) who specialized in ADHD and several other disorders. She recommended we switch from Concerta to Adderall XR, which is an extended release amphetamine drug. It is similar to Concerta, but she said some patients tolerate it better. David's ability to fall asleep and his tics worsened right away and we went back to Concerta. She prescribed an antidepressant medication called Trazadone to help him sleep. Although she said it wasn't a very good antidepressant, it's off label use was for sleep problems.

> *Off label - means the medication is being used in a manner not specified in the FDA's approved packaging label, or insert. Every prescription drug marketed in the U.S. carries an individual, FDA-approved label.*

The Trazadone did reduce the amount of time it took David to fall asleep which helped, but his ability to fall asleep was still far from normal.

The tics (eye blinking, mouth stretching and ear pulling) were making David miserable and other kids were really starting to make fun of him at school, so we stopped the Concerta which greatly reduced the tics. However, his behavior at home and at school was intolerable. Because his behavior was disruptive in the classroom he kept getting sent to the office. Having a child in the office the better part of the day is the same as not having them in school, so we reluctantly put him back on the Concerta. We let him skip it on the weekends to get a reduction in the tics, so he could play with neighborhood kids without them making fun of him. However, his impulse control was zero, so there were always problems. Also, the conflicts in our home were even worse.

My husband and I made an appointment to talk to Dr. Dorrington about the severity of the tics, his behavioral problems and the benefits and complications with being on and off the Concerta (weekdays vs weekends), etc. She explained to us that David's conditions had no cure and we needed to accept the reality of the situation. She said there were no treatments or medications that would make him "normal." She also told us that David cannot and will never function independently at the same level as other children. We left the office feeling sad, frustrated and hopeless. I had cried myself to sleep many a night, but pretty much from this point it became an every night occurrence.

David's inability to get much of anything done and his arguing everything we said was definitely a huge problem and very frustrating to deal with. His not doing well in school and his increasing tics were certainly a concern. The escalating violence towards Matthew was frightening, but his feelings of increasing hate haunted me. It seemed to me it consumed him. How could he hate us so much? We were never mean to him, never beat him (even though I wanted to on multiple occasions), and frankly, we did so much for him. I knew he got in trouble more than the average kid and he was yelled at a lot, so I understood that he might feel mad or frustrated, but hate? To me, it seemed to be building in him like a volcano. Thinking about what would happen when that volcano blew combined with his violent tendencies terrified me.

Even though I spent countless hours talking to him about his frustrations and trying to reason with him, he never felt like I was on his side or his advocate. I knew David needed some kind of an outlet for his anger, so we started seeing a life coach who dealt with kids who had mental illnesses. She immediately befriended him and for the most part David liked her. He would tell her how things were unfair and she would find a way to make a deal with him that made things seem more fair to him. For example, David would say it wasn't fair that he would get into trouble for hitting Matthew when Matthew deserved it. She would make a deal that if one time during the next week, he would come and get me or his Dad instead of hitting Matthew, we would punish Matthew for his role in the altercation and he would get a coupon for an ice cream cone at a local shop from her. It was very difficult for Steve and I, because David would create an altercation, come and get us and then not only did we have to "punish" Matthew for practically nothing, he would get ice cream. I honestly felt infuriated most of the time when I left an appointment, but since David seemed to feel slightly less hate, we continued for years.

    I always felt bad for Matthew, he was such a tolerant easy kid, but his life was difficult because of David. He got smacked, kicked, clawed and even bit multiple times. We had to punish him for small things he shouldn't have been punished for because we feared if we didn't, David would really hurt him. We didn't get to do fun things like other families (bike rides, games, movies, etc.), because almost everything we did was a nightmare because of David's behavior. It was hard enough to have a child like David to worry about and deal with, but to know it was ruining your other kid's childhood was hard to live with too.

It was a spring afternoon near the end of 5th grade and David was sitting at the kitchen counter attempting to do homework while I was preparing dinner, when I heard him make a bird like sound. I looked up and he was still doing homework when he did it again. There was no outward sign that he even knew he was doing it and I didn't say anything to him about it. It continued over the following days while he was doing homework and then he started doing it at other random times. I didn't want to ask him about it because I knew he would just perceive whatever I said as a negative comment. Since he felt so bad all the time, I didn't want to add to it in any way. I hoped it was just some silly sound that kids make.

    About a week and half later, his teacher contacted me and said he was disrupting the class by making this bird like sound in class during quiet time. He said kids were calling David names. My heart broke again because I just knew David wouldn't do anything on purpose that would give kids another reason to make fun of him. That afternoon, while doing his homework he did it again and I asked him why he was doing it. He said he didn't know and that it just happens. I asked if he could stop it and he said, "No." He said some kids were calling him a freak at school. He started crying and asked me why this was happening to him. He wanted to know why God was punishing him. I knew God wasn't punishing him, but it certainly felt like it. I had prayed every single night for hundreds of nights for help, for an answer, for a cure and nothing. I felt abandoned just like my son did. I think we sat on the couch and cried together for a good hour that afternoon.

    I made an appointment with Dr. Dorrington right away and she diagnosed David with Tourette's syndrome. She said once you combine motor tics (for David that was the eye blinking and mouth stretching) and verbal tics (the bird like noise) it is officially Tourette's syndrome.

> *Tourette's syndrome - is a neurological disorder characterized by repetitive, stereotyped, involuntary movements and vocalizations called tics.*

I know it sounds terrible, but I immediately thought of a comedy movie I had seen years earlier about a guy who dated many different women, one of whom had Tourette's and the things she blurted out were hysterical in the movie. I suddenly didn't think it was funny anymore. I asked about the possibility of David starting to shout out bad words instead of bird sounds and she said that rarely happens.

She said there was no known treatment for Tourette's. However, some people saw an improvement when they took a blood pressure medication called Tenex. We were worried about it affecting his blood pressure, but she assured us that it was rarely prescribed as a blood pressure medication. Using Tenex for Tourette's is another example of an off label use of a medication. We hated adding another medication, but we were desperate to find something to make it stop.

He started taking it right away, but it did not help the tics. He had been on Tenex one month by the end of the school year and his blinking was so severe his eyes were closed more than they were open. David said he often pressed his hands on his eyes to make it stop. He also became more negative and antagonistic. I'm not sure if it was the medication or simply the stress of the tics. Dr. Dorrington took him off Tenex and put him on Clonidine, which she said was initially created as a blood pressure medication also, but was quickly approved as a medication for tics as well. It did reduce both the motor and verbal tics, but not a considerable amount. It also made David super drowsy and he would often fall asleep during the middle of the day.

After school got out in June, David began saying "okay" three times in a row when he would respond to a question. Within a week of that first incident he was saying several words three times each time he would use them. I made another appointment with Dr. Dorrington, but before we could get in to see her, David was repeating the last few words of every sentence three times. He said he could not stop doing it and that if he tried he felt super uncomfortable until he repeated the words. He also confided in us that about six weeks prior he started feeling the need to draw any circle that needed to be made perfect. He also had to perfectly dot all "i's" when writing.

David also suddenly started having episodes where he felt like he couldn't breathe. His heart would be racing and he would be crying that he couldn't get any air. We hadn't seen Dr. Dorrington yet for the word repeating, but felt the immediate need to see our pediatrician about the breathing episodes. Dr. Hutchinson said he thought David was experiencing panic attacks, but ordered an EKG just to be thorough.

> *EKG – electrocardiogram is a test that checks for problems with the electrical activity of the heart.*

I don't think my husband and I slept for more than a few hours over the next couple days. We checked on David while he was sleeping constantly to make sure he was still breathing. He seemed so at peace at night! The EKG was normal, it was indeed panic attacks.

Even though only a couple weeks had passed since the word repeating had begun, by the time we were able to see Dr. Dorrington, David had changed. He was far less argumentative and angry and significantly more emotional, crying all the time. If we couldn't have heard his voice or see his face we wouldn't have known it was him based on his behaviors. He was saying the phrase "Yeah, ok then right," a hundred times per day and said he couldn't remember anything. Once while playing the game "Go Fish" he started crying because he forgot what he was supposed to do. Dr. Dorrington said all the word and phrase repeating was an Obsessive Compulsive Disorder (OCD) and referred us to a psychologist who specialized in OCD (Dr. Cunningham).

> *OCD - is an anxiety disorder in which people have unwanted and repeated thoughts, feelings, ideas, sensations*

(obsessions), or behaviors that make them feel driven to do something (compulsions).

Dr. Dorrington also prescribed Celexa for the panic attacks. She said the crying and forgetfulness could be attributable to many different things, but wanted to wait to see how he did on the Celexa before worrying about it - easy for her to say!

Celexa – is a selective serotonin reuptake inhibitor commonly used to treat depression and panic disorders.

David was so tired on the Celexa he really couldn't function. I had trouble getting him up after 12 hours of sleeping and he would still fall asleep during the day. He was switched to Zoloft within a week of starting the Celexa.

Zoloft - is also a selective serotonin reuptake inhibitor commonly used to treat depression and panic disorders.

He said he still felt tired on the Zoloft, but not nearly as bad as the Celexa. He went back to having trouble sleeping in spite of the tiredness.

We started working with Dr. Cunningham and saw him a couple times per week until school started. He was truly a wonderful therapist and for the first time in a long time I felt like someone besides me and my husband really cared. He taught David techniques to work through the anxiety he felt when he didn't repeat a word or phrase. Initially things seemed to worsen as David simply started repeating phrases of similar meaning instead of singular words and started to compulsively clean things. His behavior also worsened; he was wild and crazy running around the house screaming and yelling at the top of his lungs. He said he had pressure in his gut and had to yell.

Dr. Dorrington upped the dosage of both the Clonidine and Zoloft and we practiced the OCD exercises one to two hours a day at home. Within a couple months David went from repeating a hundred times per day to just a few. The crying, forgetfulness and running around the house yelling seemed to disappear and David went back to being oppositional, defiant and argumentative.

Chapter 4
Sixth Grade

By the beginning of sixth grade, we felt beaten down, exhausted and hopeless. We enjoyed very little as family because David was so difficult. Whether it was camping, vacations, family movie night, game night, bike rides, etc., we would usually end up thinking "Why did we even bother." My marriage was strained because we were both so stressed all the time and I personally was emotionally depleted and had nothing else to give anyone after dealing with David every day. I loved David with all my heart, but he had taken everything I had to give. I never ever wanted anything to happen to him, but as ashamed as I am to admit this, I started wishing he had never been born. He was miserable, we were miserable and the future looked bleak. I can't write this or even think about it today without crying, as today I can't imagine life without him.

We started this school year with David still having severe behavioral problems, academic struggles, sleep problems, anxiety, Tourette's (twisting his ear, severe heavy blinking, large mouth stretches and making bird like sounds all the time) and OCD that was currently under some control as long as we did daily exercises. He was taking five medications and we regularly saw his psychiatrist, clinical psychologist, life coach, OCD psychologist and a family counselor.

Within a month of school starting, David began rolling his eyes and laughing uncontrollably. Dr. Paul said it was either additional tics or it could be a new compulsion. He said if it were a compulsion, increased OCD exercises should reduce the occurrences, but if it were a tic the exercises would not help.

We immediately increased the OCD exercises, but it did not help. Dr. Cunningham gave us new exercises to try and help reduce the tics, but they also made little difference. Dr.Dorrington then increased David's dose of Clonidine and it did help some.

Even though we were initially told that Clonidine was not a very good blood pressure medication and was more commonly used for tics, it was enough to lower David's blood pressure to the point he started passing out in his PE class. After the second occurrence we had to remove him from PE, which was really disappointing because not only did David love PE, he also really needed the ability to run around.

By November, David's teacher requested a conference to discuss the problems he saw in David:

- fidgeting

-restlessness

-excessive talking

- impulsivity

- interrupting others

- difficulties with sustaining attention

- inability to follow instructions

- failure to give close attention to details

- failure to listen when spoken to directly

- oppositional and defiant behavior

- disrespectful and disruptive in class

He told us he sent David out of the classroom several times per day for bad behavior and that David was really falling severely behind in reading. We discussed the teacher's conference with Dr. Dorrington and it was decided that we needed to raise the dose of the Concerta to control the bad behavior, so he could be in the classroom more. The increased dose helped his behavior somewhat in the classroom, but increased his tics and his inability to sleep. Dr. Dorrington then increased the dose of Trazadone to help with the sleep problems.

By the middle of January, David had started grunting in additional to his bird like sounds. When he first started doing it, I think it even surprised him. He would almost look around like where did that come from. Once he realized he couldn't control it, it frightened him. He curled up in my lap and just sobbed. He said he didn't like the bird like sounds he made, but at least sometimes people thought they were birds and not him and sometimes kids thought he did it on purpose to be funny. He said no one would mistake his grunting for anything else and everyone would think he was weird. He said he never wanted to leave the house again and it wasn't fair that no one else had to deal with these problems. He also wanted to know why God hated him.

I cried until I didn't think I should have any tears left, but they kept flowing. I knew God didn't hate David and I told him so, but struggled with what else to say. I couldn't explain why God would give a kid so many problems because I couldn't understand it myself. I couldn't tell him it would get better, because nothing had gotten better in years; in fact everything had gotten worse. I told him that Matthew, his Dad, myself and Grandma and Papa all loved him very much and we didn't care if he made grunting noises. I told him every time he made the grunting noises we could all make them, like we had recently seen a family of wild pigs do on an animal special on TV. He liked the idea and for weeks we all snorted and grunted together.

    Dr. Dorrington increased his dose of Clonidine to try and help with the grunting, but as usual it only reduced the problem a little. It felt like we were constantly taking five steps backwards and one forward. Shortly after increasing the Clonidine, David started worrying more excessively than usual. He was so distracted by what he was worried about that his ability to study at home and at school worsened. He worried about something happening to his Dad and I, getting teased at school by other kids, his grades, the tics getting worse, etc. It almost seemed obsessive to me, but Dr. Paul said it was anxiety.

Dr. Paul said I needed to distract David when he had a tic, so he wouldn't be so bothered by them and thus it would reduce the amount of time he worried about them. This was a ridiculous request as David's tics were nearly constant! How could I distract him several times per minute all day? I was told to increase the reward system for normal behavior. I was enraged by this request; David didn't want to be the way he was, he couldn't just be normal because there was a Lego set promised. His issues were so far beyond bribing!! I was told to buy a squishy ball for him to have in his hands to help distract him from worrying about things, this also was something I felt would only minimally at best be helpful.

After Dr. Paul finished telling me all the things he wanted me to do, I lost it. I was crying and raising my voice and saying these things were not going to fix the problem, did he not see how David was getting worse and needed something drastic? Lego sets, squishy balls and me being silly to distract him hundreds of times per day were not the answer!! It was like putting another Band-Aid on a gaping wound. He said I wasn't trying hard enough! I'm not sure if I was madder or sadder in that moment. How could I be trying any more than I already was? I was probably involved with what David was doing 80% of the time he was home, whether it was homework help, redirection during play time, keeping the peace between Matthew and him, the myriad of exercises we did daily, helping him fall asleep every night, several doctor appointments weekly, frequent school meetings, etc. In addition to all that I was still a wife and a mother to another child. Every free minute I had, I spend scouring the internet for help for him. I did absolutely nothing for myself and yet I apparently wasn't trying hard enough. I reiterated that we had been in multiple forms of psychiatric counseling for years, done numerous "home exercises," attended classes, read multitudes of books, had hundreds of appointments with countless calls in between and tried multiple medications with multiple dose adjustments. We had done every single thing that had been asked of us and yet he continued to get worse. WHY?? WHAT WERE WE MISSING? WHAT ELSE COULD BE DONE?

He said many children get worse and they don't really know why and medications that help one issue often make another problem worse and there is no real solution. I left feeling more helpless and frustrated than usual.

Dr. Dorrington decided to switch from Concerta back to Adderall XR again. I mentioned that he did not tolerate the Adderall very well the last time we tried it, but she wanted to try again anyway. Almost immediately David was more argumentative and nasty, but she wanted us to try it for an entire month. We upped the dose slowly, but well before the month was over David was sent home from school with a racing heart, blurred vision, dizziness and a headache. We switched back to Concerta immediately.

In April, David was sitting at the kitchen counter doing homework while I was making dinner and he said, "amen," three times pretty loudly. It was very similar to the prior April when he had started making the bird sounds. Over the next few weeks, the bird sounds and grunting disappeared and David would say "amen" three times multiple times per day. Sometimes they were loud, but usually quiet or normal voice volume. I, of course, contacted his doctors again and was told that his Tourette's had graduated from sounds to words. I asked why he would use the word "amen" and I was told people with Tourette's do not choose the words they use, it just happens. He said David's utterances could remain the same or change. I knew David using words out loud would be more difficult for him than bird sounds or grunting, but at the time I thought that of all the words to say, this might be one of the easier ones. We told him to tell other kids he was praying. I knew this wouldn't make things ok, but it might help a little. Usually when David would get worse I would feel so sad, but this time I almost felt numb.

By the end of the school year, we had seen a gradual worsening of most of his symptoms. He was finding it more difficult to concentrate on anything and was barely passing the 6th grade. His tolerance to frustration was declining, he interrupted constantly, and was very argumentative. His hate towards all of us and his aggression towards Matthew had increased. His tics (heavy eye blinking, mouth stretching and triple saying amen) were constant. He was more anxious and constantly worried about me dying and what would happen to him. He cried almost every night at bedtime and started grinding his teeth.

My husband and I decided to leave the medical system that was covered by our medical insurance and seek other help. Besides Dr. Cunningham, none of David's doctors really seemed to care or have any answers. It seemed we had reached the point where all they had to offer was family counselling and medication increases that did not help. I researched doctors within a hundred miles of our house and chose a Pediatric Psychiatrist (Dr. Fleener) and a Pediatric Psychologist (Dr. Applebaum) that had wonderful reputations as among the best and they both ended up being not too far from us. We couldn't get in for nearly a month and in that time David's Tourette's was really kicking up. The number of times per day that he said "amen" three times had dramatically increased. It was summer vacation and David didn't want to play with other kids because his "amens" were so out of control. He didn't even want to see Timmy, who had played for years with him and rarely ever commented on the different things David did.

Dr. Fleener agreed with all of David's previous diagnoses, but immediately took him off Concerta and put him on Focalin XR.

> *Focaline XR – is a central nervous system stimulant that is used in the treatment of ADHD and Narcolepsy.*

On the first day of being on the Focaline XR, David said that he felt really bad, like there was no reason to live. This feeling went away by the end of the day, but David was completely exhausted. Within a few days his motor tics had decreased, but the number of times he said "amen" (always three at a time) had increased. Just over one week into the Focaline XR, David was even harder to get along with, very argumentative, didn't listen to anything we said, started smacking Matthew more and was sometimes super silly. He also started twitching his nose and rolling his shoulder, which were new motor tics.

By the end of July, his motor tics and "amens" were the worst they had ever been. Our social life completely dried up as David wouldn't let anyone see him. I made him go with me to grocery store one afternoon and even though it was over 100 degrees outside, he wore a hooded sweatshirt to hide his face. He was doing huge mouth stretches, constant heavy eye blinking, nose twitching and shoulder rolling all while saying "amen" constantly. Looking back, it was a total mistake on my part to bring him to the store that day. I couldn't leave him at home by himself (Matthew was at a friend's), babysitters were not an option and I thought it wouldn't be a big deal for just a short trip. We were almost done shopping when a kid, I'm guessing about 19 years old, walked by and said out loud "What a fucking freak!" David ran out of the store crying and for the first time in my entire life I left an entire cart of groceries in the middle of an aisle. I caught up to David near the car and we ended up in the back seat where we just cried. I told him how sorry I was, that it was my mistake. He said it wasn't my mistake, people were just mean. He wanted to go home, but it took me awhile to stop crying enough to be able to drive.

I called Dr. Fleener to say we needed more help, what we were doing was not working. David's Tourette's was out of control and at the time seemingly the worst thing that was happening to him. I guess he just couldn't believe how much worse it had gotten in a short amount of time, so he asked me to count how many times David shouted out in a weekend from Friday to Sunday. My husband and I took turns counting each hour of each day and by Sunday early evening we were exhausted and just stopped counting. We had pages and pages with hash marks. David had shouted the word "amen" over 9,000 times.

Dr. Fleener saw us immediately and not only listened to our description of what was happening, he also witnessed David's constant shouting, increased eye rolling, nose twitching, mouth stretching and shoulder rolling. He said there were no medications for Tourette's and no known successful treatments. He said however though in extreme cases, like David's, people like him often had some success using antipsychotic medications. David was not psychotic nor did he have schizophrenia, but an off label use of the medications were for Tourette's. He suggested the medication Invega and said it was a very expensive drug and had some possible serious side effects, but this class of medication was David's only hope.

> *Invega – is an antipsychotic medication that works by changing the effects of chemicals in the brain. It is used to treat schizophrenia in adults and teenagers over the age of 12.*

    I went home and started researching antipsychotic medications used off label for Tourette's. All of the prior medications David took had possible serious side effects, but antipsychotic medications certainly were the scariest of all. There were many possible unpleasant side effects, but the most terrifying was Tardive Dyskinesia.

> *Tardive Dyskinesia – Permanent involuntary muscle movements of the tongue, lips, face, trunk and extremities that occur in patients treated with long term antipsychotic medications.*

In most drugs if you have a side effect, you can just stop taking the medication and the side effect goes away. Tardive Dyskinesia was horrible and permanent, as a mother how could I allow such a risk with good conscience?

Our next appointment was the following week and Dr. Fleener asked if we were ready to start the Invega. I told him of my fears about the Tardive Dyskinesia and he said I shouldn't worry because it was a long term use problem and ultimately not that common. I asked what kind of life David would have if he were one of the unlucky ones to get Tardive Dyskinesia? In the middle of it all, David spoke up and said "Mommy, I want to take the new medication if there is chance it will stop the words, what kind of a life do I have now?" I felt so trapped, how could I say "no" and yet how could I say "yes?"

I asked to speak to Dr. Fleener alone, so David left the room and I broke down and just asked why? Why was David this way? Why does he keep getting worse every year? Why does nothing seem to help? He replied, but in the end had no real answers. He discontinued the Clonidine and Trazadone and David started the Invega the next day. He immediately could not sleep and had to start taking the Trazadone again.

The "why" had haunted me for years. We had asked every doctor, psychiatrist, and psychologist and there was never a clear answer. All the research I had done online also seemed to have no answer. I just couldn't accept it and wanted another medical opinion. My husband agreed and we took David to get two additional medical opinions. We had all kinds of tests done and in the end the diagnosis' and suggested treatments remained the same. We spent a lot of time, money and energy asking our "why" questions again and the answers were the same as we had heard over and over.

ADHD was believed to be caused most often from heredity and sometimes from a brain injury or from having a mother who smoked or drank during pregnancy. It didn't seem like heredity was David's issue as no one in our families had it. He had never had a brain injury and I certainly didn't drink or smoke or even take so much as an aspirin during my pregnancy. Tourette's, anxiety and OCD had no real identifiable causes even though some studies seemed to suggest numerous biological and environmental factors.

By the end of the summer, the Invega had kicked in and David's motor tics were down about 40% and his verbal tics (amens) were down about 30%. His OCD had kicked up a bit, but his overall behavior was a little better.

Chapter 5

First Half of Seventh Grade

Everything changed when David started 7th grade. Instead of one classroom with one teacher, he now had five classes with four different teachers and a locker to deal with. I met with the principal and explained some of David's challenges and he assured me the teachers would work hard to help him succeed. David so wanted Jr. High to be a fresh start with half the kids being new and not knowing him or the challenges he had faced in earlier years.

The first week of school was only a couple days long and David said he concentrated really hard to not say "amen." Even though he said the concentration only helped a little, his mouth stretches and eye blinking increased. He said he looked down a lot so kids wouldn't notice. By the week's end his eye blinking was out of control. Stress always seemed to make the tics worse.

By the second week of school, his "amens" were climbing and all his facial tics were up. He said he felt like life wasn't worth living and there was nothing he felt like doing. He also needed Ritalin in the afternoon to have enough concentration to try and get his homework done.

By the third week of school, David said his "amens" were the worst they had ever been. They were not the worst they had ever been, but it must have seemed like it to him. I'd say they were still down about 25% from pre-Invega days, but he was still saying it hundreds and hundreds of times per day. The teachers started sending him out of the classroom and to the office when his utterances became quite noticeable. They had all made a deal with him that they would find a reason to have David leave when things got bad, to help avoid kids making fun of him. At this point, I was bringing David home from school early every single day and some days he never even made it out of the car in the morning before things got out of control. He was for the most part, home schooled.

It was a Tuesday on one of those mornings where David never made it to school that ended up being the worst day of my life. Matthew was in school, Steve was at work and David was in his room playing. We had taken a break from school work. I had heard him in his room, but then realized it had been quiet for a while. I went upstairs and David was sitting in the middle of his bed. As soon as he saw me he started crying. He said he wanted to kill himself. He said he had been thinking about it for a while, but was afraid he wouldn't go to heaven because he knew suicide was a sin. He said it wasn't fair to make a kid want to kill himself and then punish him by not letting him into heaven. I wanted to tell him that I believed he would go to heaven if he killed himself, because God was loving, forgiving and knew what was in his heart, but I was afraid maybe this fear was the only reason he was still here, so I didn't say anything. I asked him why he wanted to kill himself and he just said that his world felt dark. In the next few days before we could get in to see Dr. Fleener, my husband and I never left David alone, not even for a minute.

Dr. Fleener said the depression was most likely a side effect of the Invega, but it was possible he simply now had depression and it was not related to the Invega. David was a little young for the average onset of depression, but depression is more common among kids who have other mental disorders. Dr. Fleener indicated our only options were to either take him off the Invega, knowing his verbal and motor tics would get worse, or put him on an antidepressant. He recommended the antidepressant. He asked his assistant to take David out the room for a minute and to stay with him. I was nervous to leave him even for a minute, but agreed. He came and sat next to me on the couch and told me that Steve and I needed to prepare ourselves for David's future. He said I needed to accept that David had serious neurological problems that would likely get worse. I needed to stop trying to fix it and concentrate on how to make our current life manageable. He said David would not go to college, probably not graduate from high school, would struggle with gainful employment and would have social problems his entire life. I felt sick, panicked and a deep sense of sadness.

    He had David brought back in and handed me a form to fill out. He said it was a standard form that stated that I understood that antidepressants sometimes have the opposite effect on kids and their depression worsens and they actually do kill themselves. I said I didn't understand that and wouldn't sign it. He said he wouldn't write the prescription and we left.

It's hard to describe how I felt that night, but to say I felt bad would be an understatement. I felt panicked and anxious, like the walls were closing in. I had no options and no hope. At this point we had had four medical opinions from four different medical systems, tried so many different things and were seemingly at the end of the line. Steve and I decided that nothing was worse than David killing himself, so we decided to immediately discontinue the Invega, knowing David's tics would worsen, and pull him completely out of school.

Like so many other nights, I couldn't sleep and just laid there sobbing for hours. I prayed for David as I had hundreds of nights before. My worries about his future terrified me. Even if the risk of suicide went away, David was out of control. I was already having trouble physically controlling him and Steve was starting to struggle with it too. What would happen during his rages once puberty set in and we couldn't physically stop him? The physical altercations between David and Matthew had left Matthew hurt or scarred on more than one occasion, how bad would it get as they got older? What kind of future could he have? How could he ever be happy? How could we ever enjoy our life? I felt like I was plugged into a wall with one worry rolling right into the next.

As I lay there, as exhausted as I was, I suddenly had the urge to get up and get on the computer. Instead of searching conditions (ADHD, Tourette's, OCD, etc.) or treatments for them, like I had so many times before, I wanted to research brain chemicals. I was still on the computer when Steve got up the next morning. He came in asked what I was doing and I told him I was finding some interesting facts about brain chemicals and the conditions David had.

I become obsessed with researching brain chemicals and did it 10-16 hours a day for several weeks. One piece of information would lead me to another. I had notebooks of notes, charts and graphs. I would call my Dad or my friend Jenn almost every day and sometimes two or three times a day to tell them what I had learned. They so encouraged me to keep going. They said it was sometimes hard to follow what I was saying, but it seemed like I was onto something promising. Steve, who is a really bright guy, would come home every day and sit down to hear what I had learned. He said a lot of it was over his head, but it did make sense. He also managed the kids all evening every day so I could keep going.

I could write an entire book on just the things I learned, but that's not the point of this book. The information was just part of our journey, not the destination. In a super small nutshell it became obvious that an imbalance in the neurotransmitters (dopamine, serotonin, epinephrine and norepinephrine) in David's brain were to blame for all of his problems. Obviously, that wasn't revolutionary, but the fact that the some of the medications he took to "help" the problems were actually proven to reduce some of the body's ability to create these neurotransmitters on its own over time was new information. It looked like this might be why he got worse over time and had to increase doses. I also learned about environmental factors and natural things that seemed to play a role in it all. However, I still had no idea "why" it was all happening!

I read studies that had been published about certain disorders David had and then read about the research scientists that had headed the studies. I reached out to contact five of them. Most were no longer associated with the same entity that funded the study I was inquiring about. Amazingly, 4 of the 5 scientists I reached out to contacted me. The conversations I had with these wonderful men changed the course of our lives forever.

To each one I explained David's problems, all we had done and how desperate we were. I explained how I had read about certain connections between the brain chemistry, medications and how natural things (in unusual doses) seemed to be possible solutions. However, I wasn't a biochemist and figuring it all out was over my head! Also, I couldn't understand how there could be a better way and the best doctors in the United States wouldn't know anything about it.

All four researchers (some were medical doctors and others had PHD's) had very similar conversations with me. First and foremost, they all made it extremely clear the research they had done was funded by the pharmaceutical industry (the majority of research in the US is actually done by the pharmaceutical industry) and they were for profit companies. They drove that point home by repeating it, saying it loudly and accentuating the words "for profit." I was thinking "Why does this matter?" "Who cares?" They said the only goal of the research they did was to create a product that could be sold for a profit. If something were discovered that would be helpful for a condition and people could do it themselves (like a vitamin for example), that research disappeared because there was no money in it for the pharmaceutical companies. They used expressions like "That information is at the bottom of the deep blue sea," and "That research is locked up in a vault tighter than Fort Knox." They said the mental health business in the United States is over a hundred billion dollars per year and no one is interested in making less money. I started to see why the "for profit" mattered.

I said I had never thought about the pharmaceutical business that way before, but what about the doctors, didn't they want to help? For God's sake we lived in the USA, the greatest nation in the world, wouldn't medical schools teach doctors better ways to help patients with mental illness if it were possible? They were all very clear about this too; "western medicine" did not embrace dietary, natural, etc., remedies or solutions and therefore did not teach them. One researcher asked me how much money I thought my Pediatric Psychiatrist made in a year. I said I had no idea and he said he would guess he's making $300,000 - $400,000 per year. He told me to think about how often I went, how long most visits were and how much I paid. After doing the math, his estimate seemed fair. He said, "For the sake of argument, let's say a cheap and very available cure (like a vitamin) were found for just a couple mental illnesses and your doctor was really nice and told you and all his patients about it. You could all stop going to see him because in this simplified example you all could buy your solution (cure) at say Walmart and be done. In not too much time half his practice would be gone and his salary would diminish by 50%. Do you really think he has any interest in that?" I was stunned and still really couldn't believe it, no way was a cure out there and no one was willing to talk about it because of money.

After their speeches about profitability and the availability of information, we started talking about the things I had told them about my son. First they all made it abundantly clear that they were not allowed to tell me anything that had not been published in a study.

Anything that had been "put in the vault" was never to be discussed and they all had signed paperwork guaranteeing the confidentiality of that information. One said, "If I told you some of the things I know and they found out, they'd own my first born son!" They all chose their words very carefully, but would repeat some of the things I had said about brain chemicals, medications or other options and told me to go in that direction. After all my conversations, it seemed like I needed to head in the direction of balancing my son's brain chemicals through nutrition and getting him off all his medications.

    My husband and I both dedicated an enormous amount of time trying to figure out how nutrition and brain chemicals interconnected. I'm not talking about how meat has protein and vegetables have vitamin C, I'm talking about how our bodies take one tiny element from one mineral and combine it with another tiny element from another substance and turn it into something else that ends up being one building block for one neurotransmitter. Steve commented that our bodies seemed like chemistry sets. It was complicated in a way that nothing else in my life had ever been. I had been on a roll for weeks now and was feeling like we had turned a corner and there was hope. However, we were running into a wall with the nutrition as we just couldn't understand it well enough to make something work.

I ended up finding a blog site where a mother posted about how she used nutritional supplements to help her son who had ADHD and Tourette's. She was a biochemist and had an understanding of nutrition and neurotransmitters. I contacted her and based on her recommendation, we started giving David supplements (specific vitamins, minerals and amino acids) that we were able to buy online or in the local health food store. We were afraid to take him off his other medications (except for the Invega) for fear of what he would be like, so he remained on those.

Within one week of being on the supplements, we saw improvements. His facial tics and "amens" dropped by probably 30% and he seemed a little less frustrated. His behavior was a little better and he seemed simply just a little happier. This was all great as we now had proof we might be on the right track. However, these improvements were not even close to where we needed to be. We had gone as far as we could with this and even though he remained on the new supplements, we knew we needed to do more.

I started researching other biochemists and other professionals I thought might be able to help us and ended up finding a Naturopathic doctor (Dr. Canfield) who specialized in neurological disorders. I had never been a believer of Naturopathic medicine or "Eastern medicine", but after all I had learned, I was now open to it. Dr. Canfield was located in a city not too far from us and I immediately made two back to back appointments, as I knew there would be a lot to discuss.

I did not bring David to the first appointment as it was hard to talk about his problems in front of him and I also didn't want him to possibly hear that the doctor couldn't help us. Also, it was impossible for David to sit in a chair for 5 minutes much less 3 hours and I knew he would interrupt constantly. Dr. Canfield was really nice and he listened very carefully to what I said and he asked many questions. In the end, he said he had helped many kids with ADHD, anxiety or depression get better using natural means. However, he said he had never had a case as complicated as David's, never seen a child with so many severe problems. He said he could not make any promises, but thought he could help. He indicated he would work extra hard and do the research if needed; he would learn from this case as well. He told me that helping David would not be simple and he would need a lot from me. I said I was all in and there was nothing I wouldn't do. I asked how long he thought it would take and he said that even though we would see gains along the way, he needed approximately two years.

I liked him and felt a real sense of hope, something I hadn't had a lot of in the past. I told him how anxious I was to get David off his medications and he agreed, but said we would have to do it gradually. He gave me two supplements, Neuroreplete and Cysreplete and said David had to adjust his diet and go gluten and dairy free.

Neuroreplete – is a balanced nutrient formula that supports serotonin, dopamine, norepinephrine and epinephrine production in the proper ratio. Serotonin is associated with mood, appetite, sleep, memory, learning, temperature regulation and pain sensation. Dopamine, norepinephrine and epinephrine (the catecholamines) are associated with control of movement, balance, motivation, focus, addiction and the drive for reward. It is a made up of Vitamin C, vitamin B-6, Folate, Calcium, L-Lysine, 5HTP and L-tyrosine.

Cysreplete - contains cysteine, along with selenium and folic acid. Cysteine supports immune health, normal toxin maintenance, normal glutathione levels, many metabolic pathways, as well as protein synthesis and structure.

We started the supplements that day and were gluten and dairy free the next. Within 48 hours, David's tics had decreased by 80-90%. David said he couldn't remember a time when his tics were so low! We put him back in school, but within a couple days the eye blinking was up again at least 40% and he said he was starting to feel depressed again. Another 3 days later and his eye blinking was decreasing, but his "amens" were increasing. He was also still feeling depressed and was very defiant and hard to get along with.

The next few days were like a roller coaster with certain things getting better and others worsening. Later that week, David was sent home from school for being argumentative, nasty, disrespectful and disobedient. His verbal tics were up about 10% from the prior week and his eye blinking was really bad. The next day, he came home from school because his tics were too bad to be in class and the day after that he never even made it to school because of the tics. However, the depression seemed to have gone away.

It was now the beginning of the third week under Dr. Canfield's care and David did not go back to school for the next few days as his tics were still too bad for class, but they were decreasing a little every day. He could go hours with virtually no tics and then suddenly for hours they would be bad again. He was still struggling with having enough concentration to accomplish much in terms of school work and his behavior, even though slightly improved, was still a huge problem.

Dr. Canfield and I were in almost daily communication and he added a bunch of new supplements:

Morning:

- *One more neuroreplete*
- *One silymarin*
- *One Lecithin*
- *One Acetyl-L-Carnitine*
- *One B Complex vitamin*
- *One No flush Niacin*
- *Four Glycine*

Afternoon:

- *Two more Neuroreplete*
- *One more No flush Niacin*

Bedtime:

- *One more Silymarin*
- *One more Acetyl-L-Carnitine*
- *One Taurine*
- *Four more Glycine*

Almost a month into Naturopathy and David was having to swallow 22 capsules in a day. He struggled in the beginning and many capsules ended up being spit up in the sink. We tried several different techniques and over a short amount of time he seemed to master the art of pill swallowing. It was hard on him, but he knew there was a chance this could help him and he wanted the help! He didn't see a problem with his behavior, but he hated the tics, OCD and anxiety.

Forty-eight hours into the new supplements and David's tics were way down again. He had some eye blinking in the morning and then very little after that and he only said "amen" nine times! I couldn't help but think it had only been a couple months since he said "amen" thousands of times in a day! I held my breath to see if the new change would stick. The next morning he had no tics at all, so I took him to school at 11:00am. He said his mouth stretching and eye blinking were very low all day and he only said "amen" a couple times.

Over the next two weeks, the tics remained very low to nonexistent. I had stopped crying myself to sleep several weeks prior and now I was crying tears of joy! My beautiful David with a normal face not all contorted with abnormal movements. No heavy eye blinking, no wide mouth stretches, no shoulder rolling, no nose twitching, no ear pulling and a beautiful head of blond hair.

It seemed we had conquered the tics, but his behavior remained a serious problem most of the time. Even though it seemed better on some days, it was clearly not better on others. On a Sunday afternoon, during a Minnesota Vikings vs Detroit Lions football game, David lost it when Minnesota didn't win and attacked Matthew viciously. He slammed his head into the coffee table and scratched his face bloody. We immediately intervened, but had trouble containing David, he was screaming, hitting and kicking. However, the next Sunday he and Matthew and their Dad played football outside and Steve said it was the most fun he had with the boys together in years. He said they had so much fun, laughing and joking and the boys even worked together planning the football plays against him.

We didn't feel he was at risk of suicide anymore, but he was still having days where he would feel dark for several hours at a time and then it would seem to just disappear. He could be good for days and then for no apparent reason the darkness would appear again.

Dr. Canfield said we now needed to concentrate on restorative therapy. We had treated the symptoms with supplements, but had not addressed the root cause. He recommended we start classic Homeopathic medicine which gives the body the resources it needs to restore balance.

> *Classic Homeopathic Medicine – Also known as Homeopathy, is a medical philosophy and practice based on the idea that the body has the ability to heal itself. It was founded two hundred years ago in Germany and has been widely practiced throughout Europe. Homeopathic medicine views symptoms of illness as normal responses of the body as it attempts to regain health. Homeopathy is based on the idea that "like cures like." That is, if a substance causes a symptom in a healthy person, giving the person a very small amount of the same substance may cure the illness. In theory, a homeopathic dose enhances the body's normal healing and self-regulatory processes. A homeopathic doctor uses pills or liquid mixtures*

containing only a little of an active ingredient (usually a plant or mineral) for treatment of the problem.

He said it could benefit all or some of David's symptoms and could reduce the number of supplements he had to take over time. He said there were many options, so it would be likely that we would have to try several different courses to find one that helped.

He also wanted to test David for heavy metals and food allergies (sensitivities) both of which can affect brain chemicals. We did the blood test for both (food allergies can be tested through a skin or blood test, but the blood test is supposed to be the most accurate.) He explained that if the test showed you were not allergic to a food then you were not allergic to it. However, if the test showed that you were allergic to a specific food, there was still a 30% chance that you actually were not allergic to it (false positive.)

He also explained to me that studies had shown that foods with salicylates, preservatives, artificial colors and flavors make ADHD worse in people who have it. Within a few days we removed those from David's diet as well.

My relationship with Dr. Canfield felt more like a partnership then a typical doctor/patient relationship. I liked him because what he had done had actually helped. It was so obvious he really cared and wanted the best for David. It almost seemed personal for him. He said he loved the fact that everything he asked me to do I did really quickly.

A couple weeks later (early December) the results were back and Dr. Canfield just sat there with papers in his hands and he had this look. I knew something wasn't good. He told me that David's blood work showed he had no heavy metal issues, but his food allergy test showed him severely allergic to 17 foods, moderately allergic to 34 foods and mildly allergic to 48 foods. He handed me the list and after reading the foods he couldn't have anymore, I just started crying. Yes, I was happy David's tics were so much better. Yes, I was happy his suicidal thoughts were gone. Yes, I was happy we seemed to be heading in a good direction, but I was exhausted. David was still so difficult both at home and in school, he and Matthew fought or argued most of the time and I spent hours researching everything Dr. Canfield did. In addition to this I was cooking without gluten, dairy, preservatives, artificial colors or flavors which was hugely time consuming. The idea of having to eliminate 99 more foods from our diet was overwhelming.

    Dr. Canfield's opinion was that David was probably only naturally allergic to gluten and dairy, but eating those foods for his entire life had created the other food allergies. He explained that every time one eats a food they are allergic to the body calls in the immune system to attack it. When the immune system is called in so frequently it almost becomes rabid like and starts attacking things it shouldn't, like other foods. Once the immune system has attacked another food, it now thinks it's supposed to attack it in the future thus creating a "new food allergy." Once the immune system doesn't see a food for three months it will forget it's supposed to attack it, unless it is a true allergy, like Dr. Canfield suspected gluten and dairy were. Once the immune system has forgot the foods, they could be slowly added back in over months.

He could see how upset I was and acknowledged the magnitude of eliminating all these foods for months. He said it was very difficult and most of his patients were unable to accomplish much easier tasks. He said he thought he could still help David even if I couldn't do the new diet, but that it might take longer or might not be as much. I started with Dr. Canfield in the beginning of 7th grade and he already told me it would take two years and I so wanted David to be the best he could be by the time high school started in 9th grade. I agreed to eliminate all the foods by the next week.

David was allergic to beef, pork, chicken, turkey, lamb, most fish, dairy, gluten, corn, soy, oats, sunflower, tomato, corn, eggs, many spices including vanilla and cinnamon, lots of fruits and vegetables as well as other foods. I went through my recipe box and found very little I could still make and looking on the internet was worthless. I made up a few recipes using the vegetables he could have, rice or potatoes and either buffalo or one of the few fish he could have. I figured in the beginning we could eat these meals for dinners and he could also have them for lunches with fruit.

However, I was at a complete loss for what he would eat for breakfast, additional lunch items and snacks.

I went to a local grocery store that only carried natural and organic items as well as the largest selection of gluten and dairy free foods. Most of the gluten and dairy free foods I had been buying were no longer options as they contained soy, eggs, corn or oats. I was in the store for three hours and was literally sobbing within an hour. I completely fell apart in the middle of the potato chip aisle. I had read the ingredients on dozens of bags of chips and there wasn't a single one he could have because of the oils they were cooked in. In fact I hadn't found a single food he could have within that first hour. Those feelings of hopelessness and exhaustion were taking over again. How much more did we have to do? Would he ever actually get better? How much more could I take?

An employee saw me crying and asked if I was alright and if she could help. With all humility lost, I cried like a baby and said I was failing as a mother because I couldn't figure out anything for him to eat. I handed them my list of foods he couldn't eat and said I was sure he was going to starve to death. She gave me a big hug and said we would figure it out together. Two more hours and three employees later I had a plan and a cart of groceries.

Using alternate flours and egg replacers, I made my own bread (PB&J sandwiches) and pancakes. Using extracts like peppermint and almond with alternate flours and nuts, I made snack bars. I also learned to make sauces with blended up beans and tahini (sesame seed condiment). Only David ate the new diet for breakfast, lunch and snacks, but we all ate it for dinner. Even though I had a plan that was working, it wasn't enough for us live on for months.

In addition to having to create recipes using a limited amount of foods, what I found really hard was never having that quick go to meal. Before any of the dietary restrictions, I tried to cook most meals, but like most moms I sometimes did Pop Tarts for breakfast or fish sticks and french fries for dinner and now I no longer had any quick options. When we would get home later than expected from a doctor's appointment, I couldn't stop and get fast food or have fish sticks, I had to start a meal from scratch! Making my own bread, cookies and snack bars seemed like a never ending task!

Sometimes on a Sunday afternoon, I would sit down to read the paper and then it would occur to me that I needed bread or whatever by Monday morning, which really just made me angry! The cooking seemed to take every last second I had every week. What also was frustrating was that cooking with these alternate ingredients didn't always work. I had more loaves of bread not rise than I did rise.

My frustration with not having enough time to make all the specialized cooking as well as my lack of culinary skill in creating more options prompted us to hire a private chef. We couldn't really afford one, but thought if the chef could just come up with the recipes then I could duplicate them and life might a little easier. We agreed she would make two breakfast, two snack and two dinner options for a set price. She agreed to create the meals, bring them to us and then provide us with the recipes. The first thing we sampled were her pancakes. Steve took the first bite and actually spit them in the sink. I can't be sure, but I think dog food would have tasted better! The food was all hideous and I knew there was no way on the planet, David would eat it!

I ended up just slowing expanding on the dishes I had already made to either improve them or change them some. It took a while and we had very little variation in our diet, but it was working. It was really hard and I cried or was angry a lot of the time. The "why me" syndrome was in full gear. David was a real trooper and ate the food, but not without some complaining of course!

Now that David's tics were better, we were able to go out again, but now the complication of his diet was also a nightmare. Whether we went to a friend's house, a grandparents or a restaurant, there was never anything David could eat! I always had to make him something to bring, which meant unless I had planned ahead, I had to make a meal for him before we went out. The months seemed more like years!

By the end of the calendar year, David was taking 26 supplements every day. His behavior, rages, and outbursts remained a serious problem. He had been sent home from school on several occasions, argued and fought with Matthew most of the time and was still generally nasty, hateful and very difficult to deal with. His feeling of darkness were still there, but had diminished and his OCD and anxiety were gone. His tics had increased again over the last few weeks, but were still much lower than from before we started. He even had some days bad enough that he couldn't be in school. We were certainly in a better position than we had been in when the school year started, but my feelings of hope were dwindling as it seemed we just couldn't get to where we needed to be.

Chapter 6
Second Half of Seventh Grade

By January, even though we were certainly in a better place than we had been six months prior, we were not even close to where we needed to be. Dr. Canfield assured me we were on the right track and to not be discouraged. After all, we were only a few months into a two year plan. He increased the doses of two homeopathic remedies and added two new ones (specifically targeting the central nervous system). He also added two new supplements, magnesium and omega 3.

To get a better idea of where we were, he wanted to have David's neurotransmitters tested. He explained that essentially the brain uses up neurotransmitters daily and gets rid of them through urine. By testing the urine and seeing what was used, you get an idea of what the balance of neurotransmitters was in the brain that day. We scheduled the test for the next week, but the results would be another couple weeks out.

It was a really busy month with a lot of ups and downs. It had been a long time since we had done something fun as a family, so we bought tickets to a national super cross event and prayed David's behavior would be okay. We were excited about the outing until I realized he couldn't eat anything at the arena. I could bring something in, but he was already so sick of eating the special diet and watching us all eat "fun" food would be hard on him. Also, to be honest, I wanted a break too! Cooking everything from scratch was exhausting.

I found a seafood restaurant about an hour away (half way between us and the arena) and talked to the chef on the phone about our situation. Patrick was the nicest person and asked me to send him the allergy list and he would see what he could do. He called David about three days later and gave him the most awesome options for dinner including dessert. Watching David's face light up in excitement as Patrick gave him the choices was such a joy. Not only was the meal outstanding, Patrick and the staff treated David like a king. He even got a personal tour of the kitchen! We had a wonderful time at the super cross event and the kids got along great. It seems like such a small thing to have a fun evening out, but for us it seemed like winning the lottery. We truly had had so little fun and joy for so long I think we had all almost forgot what it felt like. For one evening we were normal and it felt so good. For me, looking back on this night when I was exhausted or at my wits end gave me the boost I needed to keep going.

We started weening David off the Zoloft this month which was also very exciting. I couldn't wait to get him off the meds! We also began doing Superbrain Yoga which is a 3 minute squat exercise that is supposed to improve people's thinking and mental function.

David really liked this girl in his class (Melissa) and wanted to ask her to the movies. This was exciting because it meant he was feeling more confident and overall better about himself. It also showed glimpses of our life moving towards normalcy. However, it was also heartbreaking because every day he planned on asking her, his tics increased to the point he had to come home. We eventually had to tell him we thought it would be best for him to wait awhile before asking any girl to do anything.

Some days his tics would be so bad he almost seemed spastic and would have to come home from school, but he could do his homework with no problem. Other days his tics would be nonexistent, but his behavior would be terrible with verbal and physical assaults. The morning and night time routines remained a nightmare. In the mornings, no amount of begging, reminding or yelling would help him get up on time, stay out of bed, get dressed or eat in a timely manner. In the evenings, he couldn't get his pajamas on or brush his teeth in a reasonable time with constant supervision. It was so very frustrating!!

In February the neurotransmitter test results were in and Dr. Canfield said they were not anywhere near where they needed to be. David's dopamine level (546) was higher than the maximum considered normal and his serotonin (34) was severely low. Dr. Canfield added on 5HTP and L-Tyrosine.

> *5HTP (5-Hydroxytryptophan) is a chemical the body makes from tryptophan (an amino acid that you get from food). After tryptophan it is converted into 5HTP which is then converted into serotonin.*
>
> *L-Tyrosine is an amino acid used in the production of dopamine.*

Dr. Canfield explained that balancing serotonin and dopamine was a very complicated process. He told me to imagine a scale with serotonin on one side and dopamine on the other with the fulcrum being an enzyme that was responsible for making both of them. If the enzyme had access to too much tyrosine it would make more dopamine than serotonin. If it had more 5HTP, it would make more serotonin than dopamine. If it made too much of one it wouldn't make enough of the other.

Since David was severely low on serotonin it made sense to me to give him more 5HTP, but I didn't understand why we would increase rather than decrease the L-Tyrosine since his dopamine was already too high. Dr. Canfield explained that it seemed obvious that David's body needed more 5HTP, but if we gave it more without also increasing the L-Tyrosine it might make too much serotonin and not enough dopamine. At this point David had to swallow 45 capsules per day. It was a lot and his stomach bothered him sometimes.

By the middle of the month, David was completely off the Zoloft! There had been no negative changes as we could tell and his OCD and anxiety seemed nonexistent.

By the end of the month, we started to see some behavioral improvements. He was less aggressive, less abusive, less argumentative and his anger seemed to have a higher ceiling. Every year since the kids were small we had gone to a cabin in the snow with friends and every year there would be tons of kid issues with David always at the center of them. These friends had no tolerance for bad behavior, so it was always stressful for Steve and me to try and constantly manage the kids to avoid issues. We could never relax and in spite of our efforts, we had never been able to eliminate the problems. However, this year we spent three glorious days with no major fights, arguments or problems. It appeared the new supplements were working!!

We had a conference with his teachers to see how he was doing and they said his behavior had been a little better, but his ability to concentrate and get work done had not improved at all. His grades were bad and they were worried about his ability to move up to 8th grade the next school year.

David's tics were still present, but were not bad and were not causing any major problems. When he was excited or stressed we would see an increase in blinking and a few "amens," but nothing terrible.

March was another disappointing month as David's behavior seemed to slip back to where it had been before. He was given detention at school for being disobedient, disrespectful and throwing paper airplanes in class. He was being more argumentative and defiant at home and being physically abusive to Matthew. To say he had a smart ass mouth would be an understatement and he absolutely didn't listen to anything we said. Down deep we knew he couldn't help his behavior, but punishment seemed appropriate, so we took his electronics away. This of course didn't help anything, but it seemed like the right thing to do at the time.

While great moments like the super cross day and the snow cabin motivated us at times, they actually made things hard on us too. When these events would happen, we would feel like we had made it, the worst was over and we had suffered enough. When reality kept crashing back in and it was evident that we hadn't made it, the worst may not be over and we were going to suffer more, it was devastating. I started questioning my faith; I felt like God was dangling a carrot in front of me and then jerking it away. It all seemed like a sick game and I had started hating my life again. I actually fantasized about being killed in car accident just so I didn't have to deal with it anymore.

Dr. Canfield was disappointed with what was happening, but did not give up. He ordered another neurotransmitter test to see what was happening and the results showed David's serotonin was up to 1696 from 34 and his dopamine was up to 802 from 546. Both were now massively over the upper limits, but he said he had some potentially good news.

He said he had received a letter from Dr. Johnston who is a medical doctor, but had spent his life in neuro research. He ran a research lab that used natural supplements to fix neurological disorders. Dr. Canfield explained that in earlier years, Dr. Johnston saw patients and advised other doctors in complicated cases. However, for years now, he only did research and was essentially unreachable. Somehow he had been alerted as to David's test results and wanted to consult on his case. Dr. Canfield said he was the guru and if anyone could get David's brain balanced is was Dr. Johnston. Dr. Canfield said "I'm good and I think I can fix David, but Dr. Johnston is better and I think you should agree to allow him to become the lead in all this." I agreed and we scheduled a phone consult for the next week.

Dr. Johnston was a very matter a fact kind of guy. No "hello's" or "nice to talk to you" or anything personable. I thanked him for taking an interest in David's case and just started to say where we were when he interrupted and started talking about supplements and brain chemicals. I tried to take notes, but he talked so fast. Then he just simply listed what supplements he wanted David to take and that he wanted another neurotransmitter test in six weeks. I was disappointed that I was not able to find out why he wanted to take on David's case. Dr. Canfield surmised that the complexity or possible unusualness of David's case must have interested him. The number of daily supplements only went down by two, but the amounts of certain ones changed.

Spring break occurred shortly after the Dr. Johnston consultation and we immediately noticed a drop in David's facial and verbal tics.

It made us feel certain that the stress of school was at least partially responsible for them. He still blinked more than normal and had some "amen" outbursts, but definitely less. His behavior wasn't great, but we had seen far worse. We also were able to start adding back on some of the foods that he had been mildly allergic to!

On the first day back to school after spring break, David came home from school and said he needed a Ritalin because he was having trouble concentrating and had a lot of homework. This stood outside the norm, as David was not proactive in terms of homework. On the second day, he said his concentration had been a little better in school. That night, Steve, Matthew and I went to Bible study down the street and we left David at home as he said he had homework to do. When we got home, he was actually doing homework! Not only was he doing homework, he had done it the whole time we were gone. The next day, he again asked for a Ritalin and without any complaining or help, he did schoolwork until 1AM. This type of behavior had never ever happened in his entire life!

David's new academic behavior continued over the next few weeks and his grade point average moved up to a 3.0. One afternoon, while waiting at the school bus stop for Matthew, the bus driver (same for both boys) flagged me over to talk to her. She said she couldn't believe how much David had "grown up" just over the last few weeks. I didn't mention it previously, but David used to get in trouble all the time for bad behavior on the school bus. It all seemed like a miracle!

The remainder of the school year was the same with David doing better in school. His behavior was generally somewhat better, but on the last day of school he attacked Matthew again and scratched his face bloody. His blinking, mouth stretching and saying "amen" was still too much for David to be okay with it, but was certainly better than it had been for many years.

In the beginning of summer, we were able to add back in the foods David had been moderately sensitive to which was so nice! Cooking was so much easier and there were actually some prepackaged things he could have again. We eliminated the Concerta, Ritalin and Trazadone. His tics were almost nonexistent and he could sleep normally. His behavior was better than average, he still had some impulsivity issues, needed reminders to do things and still couldn't concentrate on anything all the way.

We got the results of the newest neurotransmitter test and now his dopamine was 3190 which was high and his serotonin was 161 which were within normal limits. Dr. Johnston added two more tyrosine supplements which made no sense to me, but I went with it as David was slowly getting better. Clearly what Dr. Johnston had recommended in the spring had made a big difference.

Dr. Canfield wanted to begin a homeopathic method called the brain protocol. Its purpose was to help the body balance itself, so it would need less supplementation. He warned us that the brain protocol would often make things worse before it made them better. It was a six month course, so we wanted to do as much of it as possible over the summer. I trusted Dr. Canfield, but I honestly didn't understand how it worked at all.

Over the rest of the summer, David's behavior was generally better, but he did have several instances of aggressive behavior. One time, he was unhappy about something during a Wii game with Matthew and he knocked him down, kicked him and clawed his face. Another time he threw ice cubes and hit me in face. Overall, his "amens" were up a little and he started repeating certain words again, but his facial tics were gone.

Chapter 7

Eighth Grade

I held my breath as the 8th grade year began. We were starting school with David taking zero medications and the worst of the brain protocol seemingly over. The first six weeks seemed great with David doing well. He had several triple "amen" episodes per day, but he said it wasn't presenting a problem at school. His behavior was good and his study skills were great. He studied three to five hours every day with no complaints and had a 4.0 GPA. It seemed like a miracle!

By the beginning of October, we had the first school conference of the year and I went in apprehensive as every prior conference in his entire life had been difficult. The principal and I had agreed to start this year with no parent teacher meetings in advance and no discussions of problems with the teachers. Also, we had agreed the prior year that all comments related to David having problems would remain out of his file until the end of 8th grade and then they would only be added if he had not improved. Because of this, his teachers had no prior knowledge of David's problems. Four of his six teachers were new and he received all excellent reviews. They said he was a great student, very conscientious, asked great questions, participated fully and was a model student. The two teachers he had had the prior year said he was a changed person. They said last year they would have described him as distracted, scattered, disrespectful and problematic and none of that was present this year. I was sobbing as I walked to my car; I couldn't believe how far we'd come!

The principal, who was so awesome and worked with us so much, saw me leave and ran after me. When I turned and he saw me crying he just gave me hug and said he had spoken to the teachers in advance and knew what a good review David was going to get. He asked me to come back to his office and discuss the progress. He asked what medications David was on and when I said none, his mouth literally fell open. He asked how that was possible and I said we moved to all natural supplements and homeopathic remedies. He said, "I've been a principal for many years and have seen a lot of children with problems and David would be on the list with some of the worst. I've never ever seen a kid turn around like this." He knew from what I had told him a year previously that we were moving from western medicine to natural and he just couldn't believe it worked!

We had done another neurotransmitter test and the results were back in and David was at 320 for Dopamine and 809 for serotonin, both within normal limits. Even though David was doing so well, Dr. Canfield and Dr. Johnston both thought he could do even better, so the supplement tweaking went on. Additionally, we still were doing the homeopathic remedies to help the body balance itself, so David could hopefully reduce the number of supplements he had to take daily.

By now we had added on all foods except for gluten and dairy and even though it was worlds better than dealing with the 97 additional food allergies, it was still difficult. Because David was doing so well, I had allowed myself to start thinking about the possibility of him leaving home and going to college, a luxury I hadn't allowed myself for a long time. I thought it would be hard for him to live in the dorms and have to eat gluten and dairy free, so I started researching how to get rid of food allergies.

I ended up seeing an acupuncturist named Naoko. She was an older Japanese woman and I can't say enough wonderful things about her and her staff.

> *Acupuncture is a form of ancient Chinese medicine that has been practiced for thousands of years. It is based on the premise that there are patterns of energy flow through the body that are essential for good health. Disruptions of this flow are thought to be responsible for disease. It is done by putting very thin needles into your skin in certain spots which influences the energy flow.*

She said she could tell by his pulse that his liver and spleen were under functioning and that it was probably a genetic weakness, but it could be helped by acupuncture. She also said allergies and neurologic problems were commonly associated with liver and spleen weaknesses. Her hope was that David's ADHD and Tourette's could be almost eliminated which would mean his supplements could also be eliminated. Additionally, his food allergies could be minimized or eliminated as well as his spring hay fever.

Over the next several months, we did see a decrease in his "amens" and he was able to get his homework done in less than the previous three to five hours per night. To us this meant that his concentration was better, so he was able to get the work done quicker. We also tried to reduce the daily supplements, but we couldn't as his symptoms would return.

In the past, we had added on gluten or dairy here or there to see what would happen and we always saw an increase in his symptoms. Generally, it was a slight increase in tics and always an increase in not so great behavior. By the spring of eighth grade, we had six months of acupuncture under our belt and David was now able to eat gluten a couple times per week with no increase in symptoms. Dairy was still a problem, so we only allowed him to have something as a treat a couple times per month. We also discovered that for the first spring in many years, David had absolutely no spring allergies (hay fever.) Where in the past, he had to take allergy medication and he was still snotty and sneezy for months.

During the second half of the eighth grade, we made only minimal changes to the daily supplements, but did continue on with several different courses of homeopathic remedies in hopes of the body balancing itself, so David could take fewer capsules per day.

Towards the end of the school year, one of David's teachers asked me to come in after school without David being present. She said she just couldn't believe the change in David from last year to this year. She said she honestly kept waiting for the shoe to drop and for David to fall apart again. She asked if I knew Mrs. Lancaster and I said I had heard the name, but David had not had her as a teacher. She proceeded to tell me about Mrs. Lancaster's young daughter who had anxiety so bad she couldn't function normally and asked if I could help. She said she didn't know what we did for David, but we clearly had done something remarkable.

At this point in our lives, we were trying to keep David's prior issues personal for several reasons. First of all, David was so ashamed of what he was he swore us to secrecy. Secondly, so far I had managed to keep a lot of it out of school files and I wanted to keep it that way and last but not least, I figured the less people who knew the less likely anything would come out in high school. I said I would think about talking to Ms. Lancaster and would contact her if I felt comfortable. I never contacted Mrs. Lancaster and I still feel bad about it today.

David's eighth grade graduation was one of the happiest days of my life. I felt so satisfied, so hopeful and so free. It was hard to look back and remember where we were two years prior in a place with seemingly no hope. After the ceremony, where I was smiling ear to ear, we took pictures as a family and with grandparents. One of my favorite pictures still today is a candid picture my Dad took of me hugging David and telling him how proud I was him and David saying "Thanks Mom, I love you." After the picture, David ran off to talk to a friend and I started tearing up; my Dad noticed and gave me a big hug and said "I'm so proud of you, you did it!"

The summer wasn't perfect, but it was really good, at least compared to our past it seemed that way! Dr. Canfield wanted us to make it through two rounds of the brain protocol (only a few weeks each this time), so we began the first day of summer. As like the prior summer, it caused some increases in tics and bad behavior. The increase in tics was only minor with a little eye blinking and maybe 5-8 triple "amen" episodes per day. His behavior was worse than recent months, but nothing like the past. There was no violence, just increased arguing and not listening.

Dr. Canfield said seeing an increase in symptoms during the brain protocol means it's working. We finished up the week before school started and the behavior and tic problems decreased. We tried reducing a few supplement capsules a day, but again saw an increase in symptoms, so we went back to where we were.

My two years with Dr. Canfield was about up and he had certainly delivered on his promise. We went from having a son who had:

1) Depression - suicidal thoughts
2) Anxiety
3) Obsessive Compulsive Disorder
4) Tourette's Syndrome - facial tics so bad he looked spastic and wouldn't leave the house and verbal tics so bad he

shouted out "amen" thousands of time per day
5) Huge behavioral problems with violent outbursts
6) ADHD bad enough that it was thought he wouldn't finish high school

to a son who had a future. Steve and I would say David was 80 - 85% normal. This might not sound great, but to us it was a miracle! Sure, David was not going to go to MIT or Harvard at this point, but we were certain he would be able to graduate from a state college. His verbal and facial tics were noticeable to those close to him, but not bad enough where anybody would care. His OCD, anxiety and suicidal thoughts were long gone. He still took longer to get things done than he should have because he was still somewhat distracted and his time management skills were still lacking. However, we were certain he would still have a normal independent life with a college degree, career and a family of his own.

Even though we felt like we were good to go, Dr. Canfield wanted more time. He thought we might still be able to make improvements and for us the big one was getting to a point where David could take less than 45 capsules a day. I trusted Dr. Canfield so much, we agreed to stay on and keep striving forward. I figured I had nothing to lose and everything to gain.

Chapter 8

First Half of Ninth Grade

David was so excited for high school to start, a whole new beginning! He and Timmy were still best friends, but David was excited to make new friends who had never seen him during the bad years. It all started out great with David loving the feel of high school and liking his teachers and classes.

I also was loving my life! I felt so free, like I didn't have a care in the world. I had lunch with my friends, started volunteering time at a children's charity and when Jenn and I would have wine we would talk about the future, trivial things and laugh instead of cry. Matthew was happy we had peace in the house and he and David enjoyed doing things together, even watching football games! We socialized as a family and Steve and I started enjoying each other. We had made it!

I checked in on David's grades online here and there and he was doing great. He had three A's and one B just a week before the first quarter end. It was a Tuesday evening and like déjà vu, I was making dinner and David was sitting at the kitchen counter doing homework. I heard him chirp a couple times and then he started saying "amen." It was certainly noticeable, but I didn't want to panic. I asked

David what was happening and he said he didn't know, but didn't seem too worried about it.

The next night, he was at the counter again doing homework and he looked up and said, "Mom, my brain isn't working." I asked what he meant and he said he could read the math problem, but it was like his brain wasn't responding. I was concerned, but again thought it must be a blip and didn't want to panic. He struggled to finish his homework and was up to 11:30PM. On the third night, he was a mess. He couldn't get any work done and begged for a Ritalin, his eye blinking was pretty bad and his "amens" were not hideous, but definitely up.

Late that night, Steve was refilling the pill containers (we used weekly pill containers to organize all the morning, afternoon and evening supplements) and he commented on us using a new supplement. I said that everything was the same and we hadn't switched anything in months. He held up a bottle and said, "I know I haven't filled the containers in a couple weeks, you have, but I have never seen this before." I stared at the bottle and it did look a little different. I ran upstairs to get a spare bottle and sure enough it was different. Everything was the same except for one small word. What we had been using said Mucuna D5 and this bottle said D5 extra.

We counted the remaining supplements in the bottle and realized we had been using the wrong supplement for 29 days! We switched bottles and started using the correct supplement that night. I called Dr. Canfield the next day and told him about David's turn for the worse. He was surprised and didn't have a theory as to why. I didn't initially tell him about the supplement mix up, as I didn't want to influence his opinion. I then asked what he thought would happen if David had been given large quantities of D5 Extra instead of Mucuna D5? There was a long pause and he said that could definitely cause a problem like what I was describing. He then asked me why, when David was doing so well, I would decide to change a supplement without talking to him first? I said, "I didn't decide to switch it, it's how your office filled it." There was another very long pause.

In naturopathic medicine, your medicine (supplements) are filled by the doctor's office not a pharmacy. When I would go in, they would fill up bag of the supplements we needed until our next appointment.

Dr. Canfield thought David would recover quickly now that he was taking the right supplement again and asked me to keep him updated. I was frustrated that after all we had been through, this had to happen to us! I was also mad at myself for not noticing; I had let my guard down and we were all paying for it.

Ten days into taking the correct supplement and David was only a little better. He was still struggling with homework, his grades were falling and his facial and verbal tics were up (nothing as a bad as we had seen in the past, but definitely noticeable.) David's confidence was declining and he was starting to withdraw in school, so no one would notice. He had started arguing and not listening again, as well as pestering Matthew.

One month into it all, we were still in the same position and David said "Something isn't right, I don't feel right." He couldn't really elaborate or say what he meant, but I knew it must mean something. Dr. Canfield was concerned he had not gotten better in a month and ordered a neurotransmitter test. Over the next two weeks as we waited for the results, David got a little worse. He could not get along with Matthew and they were constantly fighting, I was yelling all the time again, his tics were still present, I had to say everything three or four times and his grades were suffering.

The neurotransmitter test showed his dopamine levels at 1005 and his serotonin level at 6. Dr. Canfield said he had never seen this happen to anyone before, but theorized David getting the D5 Extra instead of the Mucuna D5 totally unbalanced his brain. He felt like we could get back to where we had been somewhere between a few weeks and a couple months. He increased David's daily supplements from 46 to 63 capsules per day. He explained that we needed to concentrate on giving the enzyme in his brain more building blocks for serotonin as that was out biggest problem, but also needed to increase the building blocks for dopamine, so it didn't get ignored.

I had noticed that since this all happened, Dr. Canfield talked to me differently. It felt like it was more professional and he was less open. I knew I had to address the elephant in room – malpractice. I was upset that it seemed as though the error of his office staff (giving us the wrong supplement) was causing us so much grief. David was hating his life again and not enjoying his freshman year, I was stressed to max between dealing with home issues again and worrying about what was going to happen and we also had added expenses (Dr. appts, extra supplements, neurotransmitter tests, etc.) However, the most important thing to me was David getting better again and I knew Dr. Canfield was my best option.

    I asked for an appointment without David and I told him how grateful I was for him and I promised to never have a negative reaction to anything he said to me. I wanted him to feel free to be as honest as I felt he had been in the past without worry that I would yell or blame him. I also came right out and said he had my word that we would not pursue any type of a malpractice claim; David getting better was my only priority. I did however mention that I thought he should bear some of the additional cost.

He said he was glad I had spoken to him and I do think he felt relieved. He agreed to not charge me for any appointments with him, but would not cover any costs of the additional supplements or neurotransmitter tests. I did not think this was fair, but since I had promised no negative reactions I did not argue it.

Ten days on the additional supplements and nothing had changed, except for David was now feeling sick to his stomach all day. Additionally, he had really bad diarrhea. Dr. Canfield ordered another neurotransmitter test and ultimately those test results showed David's serotonin at 8 and his dopamine was now listed as unstable. He increased David's daily supplements from 63 to 84 capsules per day.

Within a few days, Dr. Canfield consulted with Dr. Johnston about what was going on with David. Dr. Johnston indicated he felt David's dopamine was always instable which is why taking the wrong supplement had such a dramatic effect. He suggested a different supplement regimen which decreased the daily amount to 68 capsules per day.

David's stomach issues worsened and he felt terrible all day every day. Additionally, his diarrhea was out of control. He literally had to run to the bathroom to make it and this happened many times per day. It became a big problem at school because when he had to go, he had to go and high school teachers were not ok with kids jumping up to use the bathroom. David made me swear to not go to the school or his teachers because he didn't want anyone to know it was happening or why. He stopped seeing friends at all because it was such a big problem.

Christmas break was hard as we had so looked forward to a normal Christmas with the future looking great and now David was so sick and everything was so tentative. I felt like it was all slipping away and I started crying myself to sleep again. I also felt so angry!! I was angry at Dr. Canfield's office for making the mistake and I was angry at God for letting it happen. What was the point in leading us to a place that would help David so much and then just take it all away? Why show us what life could be like and then jerk it away? It all seemed so unfair!

Right after Christmas, we did another neurotransmitter test and started taking pectin for the diarrhea. By early January, absolutely nothing was better and now David had started doing large mouth stretches again. The results of the neurotransmitter test showed dopamine at 1667 and serotonin at 1214, both higher than normal limits. Dr. Johnston recommended an additional 3 supplements per day, so 71 now. We also started taking carob powder for the diarrhea. Dr. Canfield felt certain the increase in supplements was the most likely cause of the diarrhea.

A couple weeks later, David's diarrhea was better (not gone), but he absolutely hated the carob powder he had to take a couple times per day. He said it tasted like poop and he had to gag it down. I felt like his concentration was a little a better, but everything else was about the same. We tried stopping the carob powder in hopes somehow things had changed, but the diarrhea came back with a vengeance.

We had another phone consult with Dr. Johnston and I asked several questions. In the end, Dr. Johnston indicated that maybe the wrong supplement was the cause of David's current problems, but maybe not as he had seen other patients do well and then for no apparent reason take a turn for the worse. I asked if he thought David would ever fully recover and he said, "Maybe, but it could take years." I asked if he saw the daily number of supplements decreasing any time soon and he said, "No."

Dr. Johnston had a few suggestions, but they were all difficult. One involved adding on dozens of additional daily supplements, which I knew David couldn't do. The other involved greatly reducing supplements to see what would happen and then push higher amounts of certain supplements based on what happened. After the phone consultation, I discussed the options with Dr. Canfield and it was clear, he wasn't really confident either would work. He had a good attitude and said he would keep helping, but I couldn't help feeling that he was in over his head at this point.

Driving home I cried so hard I had to pull the car over because I couldn't see. I called Steve, but he couldn't understand half of what I said. He tried to help, but I was inconsolable. I knew David couldn't go on taking as many supplements as he was and if he reduced the supplements his symptoms would get worse. I also knew taking more was out of the question and I had no confidence in the option to reduce and then add back on again. I felt like I had reached the end of the line with Dr. Canfield.

Chapter 9
Second Half of Ninth Grade

It was just a month into the second half of David's freshman year in high school and I was in panic mode. I felt trapped like a caged animal. I had nowhere and no one to turn to; David's entire future was hanging in the balance. I called my Dad and cried my heart out and of course he told me how sorry he was, but he also said he knew I could do it. He told me not to give up. I asked him how I wasn't supposed to give up. It had taken me nearly ten years to finally find some actual help with Dr. Canfield, how could I turn this around in time to save David's high school years? He just said he had faith in me and knew I would figure it out.

I still couldn't stop crying, so I called Jenn who dropped everything and showed up on my porch with a hug and a bottle of wine. We talked about it all and I also told her how abandoned I felt by God. How could he show David how good his life could be and then take it all away? It seemed so cruel! She said she knew God hadn't abandoned us and there had to be a reason for all this to happen, even though she couldn't think of a good one. She said she would pray for us and told me not to lose faith.

The next day I woke up with a renewed sense of purpose. My Dad was right; I couldn't give up because if I did, David's life was essentially over. I knew I needed to find another doctor. I was done with western medicine and knew naturopathic medicine was the way to go; I just needed someone with more experience than Dr. Canfield, which I knew would be difficult to find.

I started calling Naturopaths somewhat locally and told them what had happened (a lot of them will give a free consultation on the phone). I was clear on the fact that the wrong supplement might have caused the problem, but it also might not have and I had no bad feelings towards Dr. Canfield; I just needed help for David! In the end, no one thought they could help. I think they were all too afraid of being caught up in medical malpractice lawsuit, even though in several cases I even said that wasn't going to happen.

The state in which I live is quite liberal when it comes to lawsuits, so I decided maybe I needed to look for a naturopath in a state that provides more protection for doctors. The idea of having to travel to another state regularly was something I didn't know how we would do, but knew I needed to keep searching. The first two doctors I consulted, (in a nearby state) both said they would see David, but couldn't project how successful they thought they would be. They both wanted to see David and run a bunch of tests before they decided if they would take him on as a permanent patient. I chose one and made an appointment a couple weeks out.

In the meantime, I continued to search naturopaths looking for someone who would stand out as someone who could help in David's situation. I came upon another doctor, also in a neighboring state, and called for a consultation. This doctor asked me a lot of questions the others hadn't (questions no one had ever asked) and it seemed he really knew what he was talking about when it came to balancing brain chemicals. He said he thought he could help David, but wasn't sure he wanted to take David on as a patient because of the distance between us. I assured him, I would make it work. He said he would need to see him regularly for a while (he wouldn't define awhile) and would not allow phone or skype visits ever. I reiterated that I was committed to helping David and we could manage regular flights if that's what was necessary to balance his brain again.

He said he was skeptical it could work and asked if I would be willing to move there for six months. I said I couldn't move there as I had another child, but promised we could fly as many times per month as he wanted, it was only a little over an hour flight! We could fly in in the morning, have an early afternoon appointment and still be home by dinner. After a long pause, he said he was sorry, but didn't feel it would work. I started crying and begging. I told him how committed I had been for ten years and I swore I would do everything he asked. I said he could call Dr. Canfield and he would tell him how I had followed every direction no matter how hard. He said if I was really committed I would move there.

Still sobbing I begged him to not make me choose between a sick child and one I felt I had neglected for so many years. He said he wasn't trying to be difficult, he just knew from experience that a case like this would require a lot of visits, many of which could be needed at the last minute and flying doesn't work for that. My mind was racing as to how to make this work. Somehow I knew he was the one with the answers for David and I didn't want to let him off the phone without an agreement that he would see us. Should I move and take Matthew with me? Could we say we moved, but really didn't? Could we drive there and camp a couple days every week? Before I said anything, he said, "Have you heard of Dr. William Walsh?" I said "No," and he said to google it and to think about what I wanted to do and to call back and let him know.

I was still shaking from the conversation, but immediately googled "Dr. William Walsh." His website, "walshinstitute.org" came right up. I was fascinated and literally read for hours. He had downloadable papers on ADHD, depression, bi-Polar disorder, schizophrenia, autism and many others. I read every page, even the ones that didn't apply to us. He believes that advanced nutrient therapy is an alternative treatment. Below is a quote from his website:

> *Dr. Walsh has been a pioneer in the development of advanced nutrient therapies since his collaboration with Dr. Carl Pfeiffer of Princeton, NJ in the 1980s.*

This approach recognizes that nutrient imbalances can alter brain levels of key neurotransmitters, disrupt gene expression of proteins and enzymes, and cripple the body's protection against environmental toxins. Dr. Walsh's database containing millions of chemical factors in blood, urine and tissues has identified high-incidence imbalances in patients challenged by behavior disorders, ADHD, autism, anxiety, depression, bipolar disorders, schizophrenia and Alzheimer's disease. The treatment protocol consists of a medical history, specialized lab testing, diagnosis of chemical imbalance, and individualized treatment aimed at normalizing brain chemistry. Dr. Walsh's clinical system is used by doctors throughout the world and has produced thousands of reports of recovery. His book Nutrient Power provides the scientific foundation for this medical approach, including the emerging field of <u>epigenetics</u>.

Forget the doctor that wanted us to move to another state, I wanted to see Dr. Walsh! I was so excited about what I had read and wanted to know if it would work for David. However, I kept thinking "What if that wrong supplement permanently ruined the enzyme in his brain that is responsible for the dopamine and serotonin production, could it work for him then?"

I used the contact phone number I found on the website and called. The person that answered said, "Pfeiffer Medical Center." I said, "I'd like to make an appointment for my son with Dr. Walsh." The woman, Banessa, said that Dr. Walsh was no longer with the Pfeiffer Medical Center. I felt like the wind had been knocked out of me. How could I just find this place that seemed so hopeful, too late!! She told me that the Pfeiffer Medical Center is the successor of the Pfeiffer Treatment Center (PTC) which was founded by Dr. Walsh.

She explained that Dr. Anubrolu trained in the Pfeiffer methodology, was the medical director at PTC and the same treatments were being practiced currently at the Pfeiffer Medical Center. I told her everything we had been through and how desperate I felt. All the emotion of the last few weeks caught up to me and I just sobbed on the phone. Banessa was so kind and just let me babble on about my fears that it was too late because of the enzyme. She told me of her own personal story of her loved one being treated there, which is how she came to work there. She said Dr. Anubrolu had helped a lot of people and wanted to know if I would like to talk to her nurse, Maizie.

Maizie, like Banessa, was super nice and very helpful. She explained to me how she had been there many years, even during Dr. Walsh's time, and had seen so many people helped, even ones like David. I asked her several specific questions that she answered, but I still felt a little uneasy because of the uniqueness of our case because of the enzyme that may have been "hurt." I asked if I could speak directly to Dr. Anubrolu.

Later that day, Dr. Anubrolu called me and I explained how bad David had been, how he had done well under the care of Dr. Canfield, how he had fallen apart months earlier, and how the wrong supplement was suspected of "hurting" the enzyme in his brain. She listened to everything I said, explained how nutrient therapy worked and said she thought she could help! I reiterated my fears about the enzyme and she said she wasn't worried about that. I said how desperate I was to get started right away because David was falling apart in school and was drowning in the number of daily supplements. I held my breath as I told her we lived half way across the country from her and wouldn't be able to get there on a regular basis. She said that was fine and we could get started right away with labs and a medical history. We could schedule a face to face appointment later.

I was thrilled and terrified at the same time. Everything I read on the Walsh and Pfeiffer websites made sense, but seemed too easy. How could David's seven mental disorders and other disorders like bi-polar, autism and schizophrenia be caused by a nutrient imbalance? How could taking just a few vitamins, minerals and other nutrient supplements cure mental illness? I remembered the old adage, "If it seems too good to be true, it probably is." I should have jumped on the Anubrolu train like it was the last lifeboat off a sinking ship and yet I didn't.

I spent the next couple days going over it in my head. I talked to my friend Jenn about it and she did a lot of her own research and thought it seemed like there was other research out there to support it. I talked to my Dad, who agreed it sounded just a little too easy, how could a mental illness cure be so simple and seemingly no one knew about it? However, in the end other than time and money, he said we didn't have a lot to lose.

On the second night, Steve and I talked about it as we lay in bed. We talked about what made sense and what didn't. In the end, we decided it was simple; it would work or it wouldn't work. If it worked, awesome, if it didn't we'd only be out some time and money. Most importantly we decided in the future, if we didn't try it and David's life was a mess, we would always wonder what if and that wasn't something we wanted to face. Looking back on it today, I know I was simply afraid that I couldn't take another disappointment. I was approaching the end of my emotional capacity and I knew I was afraid of having a mental breakdown if it didn't work.

The next morning I filled out the lengthy medical history form, added on two additional pages of information and emailed it in. Within a week, Dr. Anubrolu's office emailed me the lab request for the urine and blood tests. David had to stop taking many of his supplements 48 hours before the blood draw, so we stopped taking them on a Thursday morning, figuring he would be fine on Thursday at school and he could stay home on Friday if his symptoms worsened. We had the test first thing Saturday morning; so again, he could have two full days back on the supplements before school on Monday. He did okay off the supplements, but the blood draw was hard. Steve took him and they were gone longer than I expected. I was starting to worry when they walked in the door. David was white and Steve looked like crap. I said, "What happened?" Steve explained that they drew a lot of blood (14 vials) and even though he thought David was doing ok, he passed out. The lab didn't want to continue the draw, but Steve persisted that we couldn't come back on Monday to finish because of the skipped supplements. The lab eventually agreed and finished.

It took about two weeks to get the results, but in the meantime, I went to David's next appointment with Dr. Canfield without David. I was terrified to tell Dr. Canfield that I had decided to leave his care and move onto Dr. Anubrolu. I was afraid he would be upset and then if things didn't work out with Dr. Anubrolu, I would have nowhere to go back to.

The conversation was awkward and difficult, but remained civil. I knew he was disappointed, but he wished us the best of luck and said he would like to remain as involved as I would allow.

Maizie called with the results of the lab work and my head was spinning within minutes. David had tested positive for pyrrole disorder and for the MTHFR gene mutation. He had folate and zinc deficiencies and he under methylated. Results on some of his liver tests, thyroid tests as well as others were not within normal limits. She spent an hour on the phone with me explaining what each item meant and how it could be corrected. She explained it would take another couple weeks for Dr. Anubrolu to study it all and then recommend an individual comprehensive nutrient based plan. However, in the meantime Dr. Anubrolu wanted David to start taking a calcium/magnesium supplement, applying zinc cream (which we had made at a compounding pharmacy) to his leg, and start eliminating a few of his current supplements.

Pyrrole Disorder - *is characterized by an inborn genetic disorder in pyrrole chemistry causing an excess of kryptopyrrole molecules. Kryptopyrrole is a byproduct of hemoglobin synthesis. It binds with Vitamin B6 and with available zinc, thus causing a depletion of both. Zinc and Vitamin B6 are essential in supporting neurotransmitters. Elevated urinary pyrroles is a good biomarker for oxidative stress.*

Manifestations and Symptoms:

- *Labile emotions, often described as "Jekyll & Hyde" personality*
- *Low stress tolerance*
- *May have sensitivity to light, sound, touch, and texture of food or clothing (tags, elastic or material)*
- *Fears or phobias*
- *Easily fatigued, irritated, or overwhelmed*
- *Poor dream recall*
- *Poor appetite in the morning (may be prone to AM nausea or motion sickness)*
- *Light complexion and hair color compared to others in family*
- *Sunburns easily, may itch in the sun*
- *May complain of a "stitch in side"*

- *Premature graying of hair*
- *Skin concerns (e.g., acne, stretch marks, eczema, psoriasis, cold sores)*
- *Soft, brittle nails*
- *Prone to misperceptions and amnesia*

MTHFR Gene mutation - MTHFR gene provides instructions to make an enzyme called Methylenetetrahydrofolate reductase. MTHF reductase is important for a chemical reaction involving forms of B- vitamin, folate. This gene mutation leads to inefficient methylation. Methylation process is responsible for:

- Cellular repair: synthesis of nucleic acids and repair of DNA and mRNA
- Gene Regulation
- Detoxification
- Neurotransmitter production
- Healthy Immune Function
- Processing hormones
- Energy production.

Other diagnoses seen in patients with MTHFR mutation:
Autism
ADD/ADHD
Addictions: smoking, drugs, alcohol
Down's syndrome
Depression and anxiety

Schizophrenia
Bipolar Disorder
Fibromyalgia
Chronic Fatigue Syndrome
Chemical Sensitivity
Irritable Bowel Syndrome
Nitrous Oxide Toxicity
Hyperhomocysteinemia

At first I was panicked because they found so much wrong with David and after all a gene mutation and a genetic disorder could never be reversed! However, I felt relieved to finally have the "why" question answered. I had asked so many doctors over the years to explain why David was the way he was and never ever got an answer until now. I also felt very hopeful because Maizie explained how it all could be overcome!

Over the next two weeks, we noticed no changes in David even with the reduced supplements. Dr. Anubrolu then gave us an individualized nutrient program for David; she wanted him to take many different vitamins, minerals and other nutrients in very specific amounts. Maizie explained how all these different items work together in the body. We decided to have it compounded, so David could take fewer capsules per day.

Compounding - Pharmacy compounding is the art and science of preparing personalized medications for patients. Compounded medications are made based on a practitioner's prescription in which individual ingredients are mixed together in the exact strength and dosage form required by the patient. This method allows the compounding pharmacist to work with the patient and the prescriber to customize a medication to meet the patient's specific needs.

In life people often remember a specific date, not like a birthday or anniversary, but one that changed their life, like the date you were asked to be married, the date of a serious car accident or the date someone you loved died. For me, I remember March 16th and April 4th. March 16th was the day David starting taking Dr. Anubrolu's nutrient compound. He also eliminated 19 of Dr. Canfield's supplements that day with a plan that would gradually eliminate (a few each week) the rest over the next few months. Within one week, his behavior was good, he was getting along with Matthew again and his ability to study was better.

On April 4th, he came in the house after school and ran upstairs and back down with a football in his hands and said the kids were going to play outside. I couldn't even get in a "Hi, how was your day?," before he yelled "I love you" and was out the door. A second later he was back in and said, "Oh Mom, I can't really explain it, but for first time ever I think I know what it feels like to be right in the head." Before I could say a word, he was running outside again.

I felt joy in that moment, but still stood there in the doorway and cried. Somehow I just knew we had made it and yet I felt sad because it took me most of David's life to get there. Even though he probably didn't understand it and could not have explained it, the fact that he didn't feel right in his head his whole life made me feel sad. All this time, all he needed were essentially vitamins and minerals.

Later that month, we left on a much needed celebratory vacation over spring break. Within just a couple days, David had a back slide and his behavior was terrible, he argued everything, threatened us and was super emotional. We contacted Dr. Anubrolu and she indicated she suspected we had eliminated the 5HTP a little too fast for what his body was ready for. We found a local health food store and bought a bottle of 5HTP and he was better in a couple days. If you recall from previous chapters, 5HTP is a building block for serotonin.

By the beginning of May, Steve and I would say David was at the same point he had been with Dr. Canfield when he had been at his best. However, the number of daily supplements had been greatly reduced. Also, he was completely off the carob powder and his stomach problems and diarrhea were completely gone.

By the end of the school year, David had three A's and one B (his school is on a four class "block system"). His tics were very low, back to the best we had ever seen and his behavior was also pretty good. We had a few small ups and downs over the month as we eliminated things a little too soon and sometimes had to add them back and then eliminate them again in a week or two. Overall, we reduced some of Dr. Canfield supplements every week.

Over the summer, David did well. His behavior was pretty good, his tics were low and he was happy. We were able to eliminate all of Dr. Canfield's supplements, except for a little extra 5HTP. Each time we tried to eliminate it, we saw a slight increase in symptoms, so Dr. Anubrolu decided to keep him on it for the coming months.

Chapter 10
Tenth and Eleventh Grade

In early August, David started his sophomore year of high school and we felt confident all would go well. I can't really explain it, but even after all the ups and downs we had been through; somehow I just knew everything would be okay from now on. David was happy and his confidence was back. He was excited for school to start, except for the homework part!

We had been with Dr. Anubrolu for six months and it was time to run the blood work again. This time there were fewer vials, but David still passed out. However, Steve was ready this time and caught him before he hit the floor! Once the results were in, we were relieved to see that his liver numbers were within normal range. Dr. Anubrolu surmised that the large amount of supplements he used to take was hard on his liver. Based on remaining lab work, Dr. Anubrolu tweaked the compound a little.

Over the next few months, we saw a slight backslide, about 20%, from where we had been in May. He still had no facial tics and only a few "amens," but was struggling to maintain B's in his academic classes. His ability to manage his time had decreased and we were seeing more impulsive behavior, such as him jumping up from the dinner table to chase Matthew.

I was in constant contact with Maizie and Dr. Anubrolu and they either explained why we had to wait to change something or they would add a small supplement to his daily routine. They explained how we generally wanted to only change one thing at a time, so we would always know what was helping and what was not. By the beginning of the year, she changed the compound again based on what we were seeing.

Within a couple weeks, David's "amens" had decreased to the lowest we had ever seen. They were barely present. His study habits improved and his grades went up. However, we were seeing occasional emotional outbursts. One time, I wouldn't take him to a local smoothie store and he cried and made a big deal over it. It wasn't a huge deal, but this type of behavior had not been present in a while.

By early spring, we started seeing eye blinking again, so Dr. Anubrolu added on an additional supplement. We tried it for several weeks, but it did not improve the blinking at all. We went and saw her (at a bi-annual outreach that was closer to our home than her office) and she determined that the amount of zinc cream he was using probably wasn't enough anymore as he had grown so much in the past year. Within two weeks of being on the higher zinc cream dose, the eye blinking was completely gone. We also never saw another emotional outburst and never heard another "amen." Additionally, we eliminated the 5HTP and saw no regressions.

All the time we had been with Dr. Anubrolu, David remained gluten and dairy free, except for times when we tried it to see what would happen if he had it. If he would have a normal amount of gluten and dairy over a few days, his behavior would always slide to not that great and his ability to concentrate would diminish. Even though we were managing the diet okay at home, it was difficult when we were away from the house. I knew for David to be the best he could be he would need to remain gluten and dairy free. However, the thought of him having to manage a gluten and dairy free life outside of our house seemed challenging.

I called and spoke to Maizie about the possibility of curing David's food sensitivities. She indicated the process was difficult and did not work for everyone. I decided that we had come so far, why not try this too. We started with urine and stool tests and the results showed he had an intestinal yeast problem, the presence of bad bacteria and not enough good bacteria. The idea was a healthy gut may not attack gluten and dairy. He had to take a probiotic to increase the good bacteria and an antibiotic to kill the bad bacteria. He also had to take an antifungal medication to kill the yeast and go on the "Specific Carbohydrate Diet" (SCD) which is a super low carbohydrate diet.

    The medications were the easy part compared to the diet. The SCD has no carbs and no sugar for six months with no exceptions, not even the tiniest amount! This made the diet with 99 eliminated foods look easy. David was growing like a weed (6 inches in less than 18 months) and ate constantly. Dinner was the easiest meal as we could do meat and vegetables, but breakfast, lunch and snacks were horrible. I learned to make pancakes with almond flour and a snack bar with coconut flour and nuts. I thought David was going to starve to death and he went to bed hungry more than once. Several weeks in, my friend Lisa who is an amazing chef, created several recipes for snacks that saved us! I was surprised David wanted to try all this, but he said six months of suffering would be worth a lifetime of gluten and dairy, hopefully!

    By the beginning of his junior year in high school, he still had almost two months to go on the SCD diet and then he had to go a couple months of eating normally, but no gluten and dairy. On Christmas day, he was able to start having gluten several times per week, slowly increasing up to once and then twice per day.

For weeks, we saw no signs that the gluten was bothering him and then a couple months in, with him eating gluten more than once per day, we started to see a blink here and there and he said his concentration was down a little. If we backed off to gluten no more than once per day, he seemed fine.

I spoke to Maizie and she said it looked like we had improved his gut health, which meant he would likely be able to tolerate more foods. She also indicated the odds were that dairy would present the same issue as gluten. She said we could try again and redo the six month treatment, but recommended we eliminate or minimize gluten and dairy. She said David could take a specific enzyme when he ate gluten or dairy. This enzyme would work as a catalyst for biochemical reactions which break down foods minimizing any adverse reactions.

I spoke to David and he was not willing to suffer another six months of eating mostly meat and vegetables, which is good because I'm not sure I could have done it again either. We decided to give the enzyme product a try. David is now able to eat gluten several times per week with the enzyme and there are no problems at all. For the first time in so many years, I took the easy way out and we never even tried to slowly add dairy in and log the results. He takes the same enzyme with dairy meals and also has no problems.

By the end of David's junior year, he had just under a 4.0 GPA and he even took a couple AP (advanced placement) classes (chemistry and calculus). He has zero verbal or facial tics and absolutely no signs of any problems. However, the most important thing is he is so very happy! Steve and I would both say he is 100% normal. Who would ever think that saying you're kid is "just normal," would be best thing in your life!

Chapter 11

Today

David is finishing his senior year of high school and preparing for college. We couldn't be prouder or happier! We haven't had even an inkling of any type of problem in over a year now and feel 100% confident we never will. We are as busy as the next family and have bad days like everyone else, but overall I don't think the little things bother us as bad as others because of where we have come from. We feel pretty blessed every day.

It's hard for me to think back to where we were five years ago with no hope. I can still hear David's doctor's words to me about needing to prepare myself for David's future of not going to college, probably not graduating from high school, not being able to maintain gainful employment and a lifetime of social problems. I remember so clearly David's distorted face yelling out "amen" and how he wanted to end his life. We are so very thankful for Dr. Walsh and Dr. Anubrolu!

I'm still volunteering at the children's charity, enjoy reading and now that gluten and dairy are okay again, I'm cooking the way I always imagined. I try new recipes all the time and enjoy cooking from scratch again. We do a lot of social things with other families and spend a lot of time together just with our family. Steve and I feel like we need to catch up on everything we missed during those dreadful ten years.

A friend of mine asked me a while ago if I could choose between the life we have had or one in which David was just born normal, what would I choose? I actually had to think about my answer for a long time and I don't think I would change a thing. David is a wonderful young man, caring, kind, compassionate, generous and I can't help, but think some of that is due to what he has been through. I also feel I am a better person because of it and enjoy life more! However, the biggest reason I wouldn't change a thing is because what happened to us may help change the lives of so many others.

I am a true believer in everything happens for a reason and God has a plan for each and every one of us. I believe David was chosen to have mental disorders and I was chosen for the journey that followed. I didn't see it then, but now I believe that on that night when I couldn't sleep and ended up researching brain chemicals on the computer that was the good Lord answering my prayers. He pushed me in the direction of the cure and He helped me accomplish what I did. In spite of hating having to write my entire life, all I thought about for a couple years was if and how I should write a book. Each time the thought would run through my head I would dismiss it as I hate writing and really didn't want to. However, the thought never went away and a close friend of mine as well as my Dad both told me the thought of me writing a book kept coming to them too. Maybe my purpose was to write this book, so others could find the help they need quicker and easier than what our journey has been.

All the names in my book were changed except for Dr. Walsh, Dr. Anubrolu, Maizie and Banessa. If I could speak directly to certain people on my journey, here is what I would say:

To Dr. Walsh – thank you for dedicating your life to helping others. Thank you for pursuing an area of research that was not supported by the medical community at large. Thank you for teaching other doctors, so they could help others. Thank you for saving my son!

To Dr. Anubrolu – thank you for having the courage and wisdom to seek alternative approaches when you saw that your patients were not thriving. Thank you for sacrificing a lucrative full time career as an Internal Medicine Specialist for one dedicated to helping others. Thank you for agreeing to see us when so many others would not and for being there every step of the way. Thank you for saving David!

To Banessa – Thank you for all your kindness! You were always so nice and compassionate. Thank you for sharing your personal story and how you came to work at the Pfeiffer Medical Center.

To Maizie – Thank you for always being nice and so very helpful! You always took my calls and helped me understand what was happening and always convinced me things would be ok when I was worried out of my mind.

To Ken (Pharmacist at HRI Compounding Pharmacy) – Thank you for always taking the time to answer my many questions and for always getting David's supplements here on time!

To Dr. Canfield – Thank you for giving us hope when we had none. Thank you for caring and for your kindness. Thank you for all the extra time I know you put in helping David. I truly have no hard feelings about what happened as I believe it was meant to play out as it did. Thank you for being the one that allowed us to meet our real son for the first time, not the one hidden behind a horrible brain imbalance.

To Dr. Johnston – Thank you for dedicating your life to research. Thank you for your generosity in consulting on David's case.

To all the "western medicine doctors" we saw over the years – Open your eyes and see that there is something better out there than what you are offering. Be a pioneer, buck the system, challenge your peers and see for yourself. Read Dr. Walsh's book, "Nutrient Power- Heal your Biochemistry and Heal your Brain." Attend one of his seminars meant to educate doctors. It wasn't all that long ago we used bloodletting and leeches to cure infections before penicillin was invented. We gave patients whiskey and a wooden spoon to bite on instead of the anesthesia we have today. Medical treatments get better over time when doctors are able to accept change.

To all you who are reading this book - if you're reading this book then you probably have a child or loved one who has mental illness and is not thriving on their current treatment. You may be desperate and feel there is no hope. I know how you feel, I was there. Having no hope is a terrible place to be! I know what you're thinking, "This can't be right, it can't be this easy, there's no way this is possible, it won't work for my child." All I can say to you is I have told you the truth, the whole truth and nothing, but the truth. As my Dad said to me, "What do you have to lose?" Going to the Pfeiffer Medical Center saved David's life and in reality saved mine and Steve's too. I pray you and your loved one will someday soon be enjoying a "normal" life.

Good luck and God bless!

Emily L. Dillon
JourneyToACure@gmail.com

Pfeiffer Medical Center – Dr. Anubrolu
3S 721 West Avenue
Warrenville, IL 60551
(866) 504 – 6076
Website - Hriptc.org

Compounding Pharmacy we use (they ship worldwide):

HRI Pharmacy
Ken Behr - Pharmacist
3S 721 West Avenue, Suite 300A
Warrenville, IL 60551
(800)505-2842
Website - Hriptc.org
Email – Pharmacy@hriptc.org

Made in the USA
San Bernardino, CA
27 August 2019